W9-BHA-608

Mastering 5 Elements

Create better relationships in love, family, business, and discover WHY people act the way they do

Professor Tanya Storch
Qigong Practitioner Jeff Primack

Published by

www.Qigong.com

First Edition Printed April 2011
Cover Design & Illustrations by: Perego the Artist
Editors: Jenny Malik and Kai Van Bodhi

ISBN: 0982449259 $24.95

Contents

Part 1: Behavior & Characteristics of the 5-Elements

Part 2: Energy Boosters for the 5-Elements

Part 3: Romantic Relationships Between 5-Elements

About the Author

I was born in a country that does not exist anymore, in a city that does not exist anymore, and educated by a system that does not exist anymore. Who am I? I was born in Leningrad in the Soviet Union and educated by the Communist regime. I remember my elementary school teachers trying to make me feel proud of my name, "Oktyabryonok," a child of October. I was forced to believe I was born in the spirit of the "great October Socialist Revolution" and the sole purpose of my existence was to spread this great revolution to the farthest reaches of the Earth. I was trained to "love" a little metal star with the face of the "grandpa Lenin" in the middle. It was pinned to my uniform at all times and to lose it was the most shameful thing I could do.

God saved me from this political social madness by leading me to a master teacher highly trained in Qigong and Daoist psychology. Through years of training, I developed my intuitive psychic abilities and connected with the natural powers of the 5-Elements. I learned how to predict human behavior, save energy from being lost to conflicts and how to increase the energy in my body using mind-body practices.

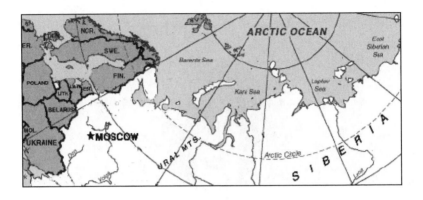

My 5-Elements education began with my early childhood experiences within the Ural Mountains. These mountains serve as a natural geographic divide between the European and Asian parts of Russia. Each summer, between the ages four and ten, I was taken away from my family in Leningrad and forced to stay for three months with my grandmother in a village of the Votyak people. The Votyak were a small ethnic minority settled near the Urals, who secretly practiced an ancient religion based on the veneration of natural forces. Children in the village barely spoke Russian. They had very little food to eat and almost no clothes to cover their sun-baked, skinny bodies. They were used to running many miles barefoot on harsh ground each day. They knew how to deal with animals, both domestic and wild, but for me this Votyak world presented many challenges. I needed to know what these children wanted from me even though they could not really talk to me. I needed to know which animals were really dangerous and which ones were only pretending. The need to survive in this entirely foreign universe changed me profoundly. Invisible psychosomatic forces, which lay dormant within me while I was a regular city kid, suddenly sprang to life.

Fire was the first natural element that presented itself to me. One day a village boy said something humiliating about me, making everybody laugh. In the blink of an eye, my internal Fire swung from zero to two hundred degrees. It leaped out of me as I attacked the boy, screaming like a mad goose, blindly grabbing anything laying on the ground to throw at him. The children ran away and never said anything offensive to me again. Anytime I turned my fire on that summer, the victory was always mine. Until one boy named Volodya, helped me discover the second element which was just as natural to him as it was deadly to me.

Volodya was the quietest boy in the village, and even girls were louder and more aggressive than him. He liked to hang out by the river, lake or swamp, and was very observant. He knew all our secrets, including mine. He took me to the pond where women usually busied themselves washing the family clothes, but on this day it was empty of people. He said to me, "If you are Fire, you will drown in this pond." I jumped in as I replied, "No, I will not!"

What happened there, at the bottom of that greenish-grayish, very scary body of water, I will never forget. I did not know how to swim because the mystery of Water had not presented itself to me yet. I had to use my innate Fire to counter act the dangers of the Water. I started to jump. I jumped for my life. Every time my feet touched something hard, I pushed myself against its surface, and as I did my head moved out of the water for a few seconds as I gulped air and continued jumping until I jumped myself out of the pond. The moment I was out, I gave Volodya the beating of his life. Then we forgave each other and became friends. He was my first Water-friend who taught me how to swim and love Water.

I was still in the vast rolling wilderness of the Ural Mountains when I befriended two more elements, Metal and

Tree. Metal was my second natural element. This is how I knew it; after every one of my fights with domestic animals or village kids, I went to my grandmother explaining why I did it. I insisted I was not a bad girl that I just needed to defend myself and pursue justice. Children did not understand why I had to tell my grandmother all this. Then I explained to them that I wanted my grandma to think that I was a hero. Later my Daoist Teacher explained to me that people with a strong Metal element always want to feel like heroes.

Another way in which the power of Metal opened itself to me was through money. Money is quintessentially a metallic force in human life and this is why in all countries, currency used to be secured by gold reserves. Because my natural Metal was so strong, I was able to keep all my allowance and not spend them on small things. When I developed passion for something, I always had enough money to buy it because, as a native Metal, I knew how to wait and count, wait and count, until I got exactly what I wanted.

The nurturing, loving power of the Tree energy came to me later. It came through the charitable actions and emotions of compassion and sympathy I felt for those hungry, half-naked kids, whose education was so poor they could not write my name or address, making it impossible for them to send me any mail when I was away. This energy surprised me because it felt so different from anything else I felt before. As I gave a Votyak friend my best dress, telling her I didn't need it, insisting she could have it, she just stood there, not knowing how to respond, something moved in me at such a deep level that I can only think about it in terms of "internal revolution."

Meeting with the Earth element happened to me naturally every year in September when my adventurous summer was over and I returned to Leningrad to settle for the winter, full of school life. I did not like that energy but felt too grounded and sleepy to change it. I learned later this is how the Earth element holds us together. It provides balance, but differently for each person. If we are not spiritually evolved, it keeps us in peace with the world through boredom and our slavery to customs and routines. If we are evolved, it holds us in a circle of love and sacred unity, allowing us to see that everything and everyone are equal, beautiful and necessary for the entire world to exist.

Much fuller knowledge of the 5-Elements was a result of ten years of training with a Chinese Daoist teacher, who himself was a political refugee from the Communist China. He taught me many things, among them a parallel tradition using the Earth element. Earth traditionally appears only once in a complete cycle of natural forces transmutation known as 5-Elements. Most people today know about this cycle – Water gives power to the Tree; Tree gives power to the Fire; Fire gives power to the Earth; Earth gives power to the Metal; Metal gives power to the Water. After that the cycle repeats itself again.

My Teacher, who is still alive, does not want me to say too much about him. This is why this account of him must be concise and elusive. I can say that he was trained as a hereditary Daoist master in a family which preserved secret teachings about Dao, Yin-Yang, 5-Elements, Qigong, and herbal remedies for hundreds of generations. During the Chinese Revolution, an oracle advised him to marry a Russian woman and escape, so his knowledge could be preserved and spread around. He successfully escaped, avoiding torture which befell other men in his family. Because of his great talents, he became a language instructor at the Leningrad University. His official obligations involved teaching linguistics and culture, but he was willing to secretly educate those students who were eager to acquire practical knowledge of Chinese traditional philosophy and medicine.

One day as I came to class late and unprepared, he told me to wait for him after the class. I thought he was going to rebuke me for not being prepared. Instead he said, "Your natural element of Fire is suppressed, this is why you lately feel tired and depressed." I immediately remembered one of my childhood games, where I pretended to be blaze of Fire, capable of burning everything. I asked him if this was what he meant. He said, "Yes." Then I asked him, "But how does one act like Fire when one is a grown-up person who must follow rules of the adult society?" He explained that there are many, many ways such as competitive sports, running long distances, singing, screaming, reciting poetry in the shower, dancing naked, rolling in mud and snow, walking fast in the rain without a hat or umbrella, and so forth.

At first I thought him crazy because it was a long time since I did anything of the sort. But as my depression continued on, I finally tried his advice. First I went skiing alone, then I tried everything he told me to do and I could not believe my transformation! As soon as I rediscovered my native element of Fire, I was happy again. My innate, sharp intelligence immediately returned. I knew the answers to all the questions in each class I took. I read every chapter each professor assigned, remembering every word. My skin and eyes shone, I was flying like a big bird.

The training continued for ten years and included numerous meditations, Qigong exercises and demonstrations of the Qi flow through seemingly ordinary events. The most precious gift my Teacher gave me was in the middle of my training; he connected me (a wild atheistic teenager) to God. He referred to God as the "ultimate master of all elements" explaining that without this vital connection, a person who had mastered all the elements may become a monster. I was actually very surprised that he had to bring God into the Daoist training. But as it turned out, my Teacher was secretly practicing Christianity; which at that time was far more dangerous than teaching about the Qi flow and 5-Elements. I remember clearly one day he asked me, "What is a Russian word for God?" I said, "Bog." He said, "Good. Now, do you know a Latin name for God?" I said, "Deo." He said, "Good. And what is a Chinese name for God?" I said, "I don't know." He said, "It is Dao."

After that he had me consciously return to all my childhood experiences, as well as my most recent Qi-power practices and ask myself, "Why did the Creator give me these amazing experiences and abilities?" I could not answer this question at the time but I can now. I know the True Source, Creator of All Life, gave them to me so I may help other people learn how to respect the natural energies which God created. And by doing so, stay healthy, living longer lives on this beautiful planet.

Before I finish, I do wish to share with you some exercises my Teacher gave me because they were so intense and effective in developing what some call human paranormal abilities. In the beginning I was not able to recognize that I became paranormal. I did realize though how distinctive I was from everybody else, because all of the sudden people became afraid of me. One exercise consisted of sitting each day in a dark closet for five or six hours with eyes closed and crossed under tightly shut eyelids. The goal was to search for the true source of light that must shine brightly from within, from the heart and mind connected to the Universal Light Divine. I greatly enjoyed this exercise and was able to conduct it very successfully. As a result, I felt at home in a dark forest or any other place without natural or artificial source of light. Additionally, my vision improved dramatically and I was able to read and watch movies without my glasses. Not only was I able to see through physical darkness but I was also able to see through the "darkness" of people's thought processes. That is to say; I found myself being able to read people's minds, quickly recognizing their true intentions, as well as hear the unspoken words developing in their brain in response to a situation. This was not scary to me, but it was for everyone I knew. Even in my present stage of life when I am trying to release some of my "magic" abilities, I still often scare people. As soon as we begin a conversation, they develop an uncomfortable feeling that I know everything about them that somehow, I am inside their brain, hearing everything they really think about themselves and the world around them.

My wonderful Chinese master was not the only God-sent Teacher who blessed my life with so much knowledge. Other great influences came from the Russian Orthodox Priests and Buryatian Buddhist Lamas. All forms of religion were persecuted by Russian communists, this is why Christians and Buddhists supported and encouraged each other during that time. They hoped their united prayers and meditations would help destroy the great evil, the dictatorship of the U.S.S.R. I recollect some joined Christian-Buddhist meditations with great fondness. One particular form was practiced in front of the TV when the entire Politburo was in session. Participants, myself included, sat in a row on the floor in front of the TV praying for people shown on the screen, sending them divine light and healing. I remember being overwhelmed with surprise when I realized that as a result of this peaceful and loving meditation, the higher members of the Politburo began leaving the planet one after another.

In Lamaistic Buddhism and Orthodox Christianity, the human body is viewed as a temporary temple filled with eternal love and light, our spirit and consciousness. Purification of the temporary temple is viewed as high priority. This is why, urged by my new clergy friends, I tried several rather challenging forms of physical-spiritual purification, including going for days without food. I practiced various purifications such as; consuming only a bowl of rice per day for five months, walking barefoot in deep snow, swimming in the middle of winter in water surrounded by ice, and lying dead on the hard floor for eight to nine hours (long enough for the soul to completely leave the body and travel to distant stars and other planets).

For me the ultimate test of the 5-Elements theory lies within the knowledge that under the graceful guidance of our Creator, I endured arrests, interrogations and other forms of political persecution in my country and I managed to avoid becoming a disabled or bitter person. This unique, ancient knowledge was also instrumental in creating conditions in my life allowing me to run away from the Soviet Union with my two little children. It helped me keep my faith and remain hopeful as my family went through several phases of immigration in Austria, Italy and the United States. Finally, it was the vision that I must share the knowledge of 5-Elements with as many people as possible that led me to build successful careers in several American universities. Keeping peace with God, respecting all He created, and wisely using my innate Fire has made my life bloom to the fullest, despite my age and injuries. I live without fear or other negative emotions and am grateful to the Creator and all life. The abundance of the life-force, which Chinese call Qi, Japanese call Ki, and Christians call Spirit, makes all types of miracles possible. Miracles are to be expected on a daily basis because life is miraculous and mysterious in its very essence and structure. When one understands the 5-Elements, one understands one's own bio-magnetic field and its unique vibrations. By taking good care of one's own nature one learns how to respect other's lives and hold everything that is life in perfect balance. In this way, our supply of Qi and Spirit will be abundant under all circumstances, making a long and healthy life reality for all people and life forms on this planet.

Forward

By Qigong Practitioner Jeff Primack

I met Professor Tanya Storch for the first time at the University of Florida in 1998. She was teaching classes in Daoism and Buddhism and I thought these courses would be a nice break from my traditional business administration classes, which were putting me to sleep. In my first class she seemed really smart, but I saw something was different about this 6-foot tall woman with huge blonde hair that seemed to shoot out of her head. During the very first Daoism class she spoke about "lucid dreaming". It's when you become aware you are dreaming *while still in the dream*. One can pick up objects and consciously investigate their nature, ask people questions, fly above the city at night, etc. For sure I thought it strange that a university professor spoke about such matters.

My knowledge was extremely limited at the time, as I had been practicing Qigong solely from books for only two years. I was confused and felt lost at times. I was having intense dreams of flying in outerspace, waking up vibrating from head to toe, and waking up in my bedroom seeing my body still sleeping etc. I was experiencing a lot of the dream phenomena she spoke of and was determined that Tanya would become my teacher. My roommates didn't understand and I had nobody else to talk to about such bizarre matters.

Tanya soon began appearing in my dreams. In one dream I was playing baseball when out of nowhere, as I slid into second base, a door appeared with Tanya walking through it. It immediately made me realize I was dreaming. I said, "Hey! What are you doing here? This is my dream!"

Needless to say I aggressively wanted to question her about this in the real world, so I carefully thought out a strategy. After her class was over I asked if we could talk privately for a few minutes. She gathered her things and we sat outside under a gigantic oak tree. I told her about my dreams, the energy I was experiencing, about all my personal problems etc. This poor woman got sucked into a two-hour discussion with me.

At the end of our conversation she informed me that my "Tree Energy" had been injured and my liver needed healing. Her advice was to go hug some trees out in the forest, which I thought was really stupid. She gave very unclear, mysterious answers to all my questions, yet I still wanted her to accept me as a personal student. I asked her, "Will you be my personal teacher?" With roaring laughter she said, "Absolutely not. You have not followed my advice and I can tell you think it's silly." She ended our meeting rather abruptly to go have coffee and donuts with someone more important than me.

My ego was hurt that she wouldn't take me as a personal student, but I also realized she had already helped me a lot with that one meeting. There was a forest behind my apartment so I entered it, finding a tree that called to me. The tree was large with parasitic vines sucking the life out of it. I ripped off all the vines that were taking its Qi and asked the tree if it would be my friend. It didn't answer. So I hugged the tree for an hour and did my Qigong breathing. Its cold bark against my belly felt healing and after a while I could feel I was exchanging energy with the tree. Each day for nearly three years I visited the same tree. He became my friend that never said anything. Listening to forest leaves blow in the breeze was a medicine I never thought to take.

After my first time hugging the tree I immediately reported back to Tanya with my progress, "Can we speak for a few minutes?" I asked when class was over. She took me outside again underneath the large oak tree on campus. "Did you follow my instructions?" she asked. After I told her what happened, she supplied me with another exercise. She told me to let go of my problems and past injuries from people that had wronged me. Her instruction was to lie down in a river, and forgive each person I held resentment against. Her thinking was that allowing water to cleanse my aura would help me forgive past transgressions.

The following week after practicing her exercise I reported back to her, and knowing I needed it, asked for more advice. My classes with Tanya and our private conversations under the oak tree were the only moments I looked forward to anymore. I completely lost interest in business finance, which was my major, and I was struggling to maintain focus with it. My Buddhism classes with Tanya spoke of "non-attachment", especially to material items, as the central philosophy of all great masters. I so badly wanted to become a master myself. So I did what any man in my situation would do having found such an iconic, powerful teacher to train with. I begged her to be my teacher. She refused. I knew she had taken on a few students to even greater levels than me. I questioned what and why she was holding back from me.

Next semester I selected two courses professor Storch was teaching, Confucianism and Eastern Religions. She always kept her students on the edge of their seat, listening with such enthusiasm. I imagined that she was everyone's favorite teacher. Amazingly nobody else seemed to be as much of a pest as I was. After most classes I would request a meeting under the oak tree. Usually she agreed and would give me great wisdom that applied to my personal situations.

At the end of every such meeting I asked her to be "my teacher". Every time she refused.

One day I was walking on the busy campus when I saw Tanya in the distance. She was dressed in black leather pants and black boots. We were both walking towards each other, but she did not see me. I was standing across the street waiting for her to see me, when suddenly she stuck her foot down 6 inches into freshly wet cement in a newly constructed sidewalk! Her foot was absolutely covered in wet cement. Standing directly in front of her I tried not to laugh, but I couldn't hold back, I cracked a laugh, and when she looked up from her feet I was the first person she saw! "How could you not see the curb was wet cement?!" I blasted. Startled by my presence she immediately roared with laughter as if it was the funniest cosmic joke she'd ever heard. Suddenly she said, "Do you know what this means?" "That you're going to go home and change shoes?" I said. "No!" She said, "This is a true sign of great significance! Please come by my house for tea."

I was shocked because I knew that she was accepting me as a student. Her big house was without a single piece of furniture. Her only possessions in the house were two chairs near the fireplace. We would sit and drink tea sometimes wine, discussing dreaming techniques and advanced psychotherapy methods using 5-Elements. She slept on the floor and was truly without material attachment. I had never seen anyone really living this way in America. Most impressive of all was that she never asked me for any money. All of her teaching was given free. This is partially the reason why I charge so little for my Qigong seminars.

Being in the right place at the right time seems to be the secret of life. After two more years of study both on and off campus I received a degree in Eastern Religion and it was during my last semester that my great teacher left the

University of Florida and moved to the West coast. Before our time was over she initiated me deeply into 5-Element theory. I saw everything in terms of the elements and was able to help a great deal of people with it. Over the years I shared her unique variation of 5-Elements with over 20,000 people in live seminars. Little did she know what kind of influence she had by training me.

Right after she left Florida, I dedicated my life to Qigong. Supreme Science Qigong Center was born in 1999 and I began flying in masters from China, Canada, Europe and elsewhere. Tanya had set the bar so high for me. Anyone we brought in for a seminar had to have been training for 50 years or more. Most of them could not speak English very well, but I learned what I needed from each master. Tanya's wisdom, combined with my Qigong training have both shaped how I teach to this day. I longed to give back the energy she gave me and to share even a fraction of what I learned from her.

Tanya never wanted to learn my Qigong or Food-Healing methods. I was forever "her student". So it felt strange when she finally asked me to teach her Food-Healing in 2005, because our student-teacher dynamic was so fixed. Now Tanya practices the 9-Breath Method, teaches our Qigong to some of her college students and drinks smoothies from our Food-Healing program. She no longer has doughnuts, coffee or wine. It's nice that I eventually got to give something back to her.

Every so often Tanya comes to visit or I fly out to see her. We are still close friends after all these years. She says she is proud of me for what I have accomplished, bringing the ancient healing arts to so many people. Yet the truth is it took one person to introduce me to the path; one person to show me by example what it means to give your life to something greater. That person is Tanya Storch.

Her students have been asking her to write this book for decades. After all these years of waiting, it is finally here. Thank you Tanya, for asking me to help you with your book. It is my honor to know you, and to serve in its creation.

A final note is in order about my role in the writing of this profound book. Many people will assume I wrote it so I want to accurately explain my role. In my opinion, this book is the single clearest transmission of the 5-Elements ever written. Bold statement I realize. I *wish* my talent were such that I could have written such a masterpiece, but only one person could possess a profound enough understanding of this subject to pull it off and that is Professor Storch. She is humble and will say we wrote this book 50/50, but that is not true. I merely refined her writings to make them cleaner and more structured. After teaching this material for over 10 years – I thought I understood it. Through writing this book with Tanya I realized I had not learned it at anywhere near the level she actually understood it. We are truly blessed that such a transmission has come into written form. No one needs private meetings with her under the campus oak tree anymore, because it is ALL here in far more detail than I ever imaged possible. Reading this book is like studying with the master for decades and if you use even a fraction of this practical knowledge -- your way of looking at people, business, love relationships, and all of life will be enhanced.

Part 1

Behavior and Characteristics of the 5-Elements

We begin by knowing what element we naturally are. In the past, this decision was made by a Chinese astrologer and physicians based on the year, month and day of a person's birth. This is how it is still done everywhere in Asia and Asian-American communities. However, after many years of researching and practicing this method, I have found that for Westerners, 5-Elements works much better if people come to their own conclusions about their primary and secondary natural elements. In chapter six I explain this in further detail. For right now, it will serve you better to concentrate on finding your own element based on self-observation, self-analysis and basically looking at how you actually behave in real life.

In the following five chapters of this book, you will find five psychological portraits corresponding to the natural behavior of Fire, Water, Tree, Metal and Earth people. Read the descriptions carefully, deciding for yourself which of the portraits describes you best. If you are a little bit confused, ask your friends and relatives whether certain characteristics apply to you or not. We all need to do this because it is hard to recognize traits of our own character.

Please do not look at what you are about to do as some form of personal labeling. It is not! It is simply a new and ultimately exciting way, of looking at yourself and connecting to your own energy patterns. The goal is to understand and experience all the elements God has created for us in this life-time and on this planet. But first you must begin by understanding your own natural forces and innate strengths and weaknesses. Everyone's brain is different and each finger leaves slightly different prints. If you are born as a water-person, you *really* experience the world differently from your fire-boss or your metal-girlfriend. You must understand these differences between yourself and other people in order to be able to get along with all of them and not feel frustrated all the time. We are all equal, but we are not the same, this is just how we are created! Good luck with choosing your own elements!☺

Chapter One

Fire People

Although traditionally the 5-element cycle begins with water, I begin by painting a portrait of a fire-person, because they can be very impatient. If I don't give them immediately what they want, they might just quit reading our book altogether. Water has lots of patience, therefore, the water-readers are going to be easy going and are patient to wait. Our Western culture is absolutely in love with the element of fire. To us it is the most romantic, enchanting and fascinating energy. In our thoughts and actions we glorify passion that burns forever, overcoming all obstacles. Almost all our great love and victory stories are built around a hero with an inexhaustible supply of fire-energy in her or his character, and virtually all our Hollywood celebrities are a fire-archetype. I invite you to look at the characteristics of fire and decide whether you too, belong here.

I. FIRE PEOPLE ARE OFTEN VERY IMPATIENT AND HATE WAITING.

Imagine you are in a doctor's office waiting in line and you see a person jumping in and out of his chair, asking lots of questions to the office personnel, talking on a cell-phone in a voice so loud, everyone can hear, and is trying to make contact with other patients who are quietly sitting or standing in line. Well, you are observing a typical fire-person's behavior. In general, fire people are very impatient and waiting *kills* them! Fire people must always be doing something, feeling busy all the time. Sitting without action and waiting for something, no matter what, is one of the worst punishments.

Here is how a fire-person named Marc puts it: "I simply cannot wait. I hate waiting. I would rather have terrible things happen to me, (then I know how to act) than to just sit and wait for something. Every time I go to the airport, I take a bag full of stuff which keeps me entertained while I wait. And on the airplane I try to talk to everyone who will talk to me. I know it's ridiculous, but otherwise I am so bored I literally feel like jumping out of the plane!"

II. FIRE PEOPLE LOVE DANGER.

Yes, they do! If you have a friend who always talks about doing crazy things and actually does lots of crazy things, that person's life is definitely ruled by fire-element. Robert describes his desires for a dangerous life, "Ever since I was little I always did what other kids were afraid of doing. I would go to a cemetery and pretend I was going to spend the night there, then scare all the kids in the kindergarten with my stories about ghosts and vampires. When I grew a bit older, I skate-boarded in the craziest places you could imagine, even on the roof of my house. I broke my left arm twice, but it didn't stop me from skating. Now I am in college and when we get drunk, my friends lock me in my room, because I once jumped off the roof into someone's swimming pool and they all got in trouble because of me. Another time I set off all the fire-alarms in our dorms and they got in trouble again, but I ran away and no one could find me..."

Maybe you don't feel exactly like Robert, but if you normally enjoy doing things that border on risky behavior, such as driving too fast in rain, on ice or on a narrow winding; if you like talking to strangers or heading out of

4

People with a strong fire disposition love adrenaline

town on a minutes note; if you like to shoot fire weapons or say things to people that you know will often burn them, but feel like saying it anyway, you definitely have your own share of the fire in your blood.

III. FIRE PEOPLE MAY QUICKLY BECOME PASSIONATE ABOUT SOMEONE OR SOMETHING, BUT THE PASSION DOESN'T LAST LONG.

Fire-people are actually capable of falling in love with a person, language, profession, or prospective place of residence in one day, or less. They can feel longing and pain of separation from people and things which attract them, immediately after they see them. When they like something or someone, they feel ready to engage in action 100% without really weighing all the pros and cons of the situation. All fire people engage very quickly, preferring their life affairs to be conducted in quick, passionate and an unscheduled manner with everything occurring at once, where no one knows what may happen next. They do not like to wait, so they will usually not wait for the right thing or person, but instead will try as many options as they can. All the while they discover that trying and changing people, and situations, is what they enjoy the most.

Elizabeth, gives us a description of what it means to be a young fire-person searching for her major in college; "I declared acting as my major because I wanted to be a celebrity. Once I realized what acting really was about – lots of repeating of the same stuff over and over again—I got very bored. I switched to the International Studies because I thought I would get to travel a lot if I had this degree and I actually liked it a lot in the beginning, but then I could not pass the math requirements and did not get to travel abroad. I got mad and dropped out of college. Then, I enrolled again and got into photography. I am very excited about my professor and my new camera and that I get to go everywhere and take pictures looking like a professional, but something is telling me that I may get bored with this too…so, I don't know what my real major should be…"

IV. FIRE PEOPLE ARE STRONGLY DRAWN TO THE OUTSIDE WORLD AND FIND IT HARD TO STAY INSIDE FOR LONG PERIODS OF TIME.

Fire-peoples' dependence and sense of wellbeing from time spent outdoors, is roughly the same as your fire places dependency on the flow of oxygen to its flames. If you stick lots of bricks, concrete and glass in between your firewood, leaving little or no room for fresh air, the fire will soon die. And so will a fire person, metaphorically speaking of course! Fire-people must be out of buildings for several hours a day just to keep their energies high and stay healthy. In this alone, they are so unlike the other elements that these people often don't understand the fire's actions. Especially water-people, who can be genuinely happy staying inside for the entire day, or even several days in a row. The may have a hard time relating to the fire person's urge to get out of the house a few minutes after they become awake. In fact, fires prefer to sleep outdoors if they can. But if they cannot, they must get outside of the house to enjoy their mornings and be somewhere, no matter where; to get coffee, to jog, to walk, or to meet someone. Just be outside. This they must do even if they live inside a house with a person they love dearly. This particular trait of the fires' makes their permanent employment situation difficult in this society because they cannot stand being in the office from morning to evening and therefore cannot easily hold a steady job without a strong dose of *metal* discipline.

VI. FIRE PEOPLE NEED A STRONG CHALLENGE, LOTS OF SUPPORT AND PERSUASION OR NICE DOSE OF METAL DISCIPLINE IN ORDER TO FINISH WHAT THEY STARTED.

One of my fire-students wrote, "I need to hate something really hard or be constantly reminded of why I decided to do something in order for me to finish the project. One time, I hated my chemistry professor so much that I got an A+ in his class, only because I could not think about anything aside from him thinking that I was stupid and couldn't comprehend the subject he was teaching. But other times it was because of my sweet girl friend that I got things done and accomplished. It was like she was a tree that gave me her wood to burn for inspiration. She would always tell me how smart I was and how she liked reading my papers when they were finished. She was a really great influence on me and I got a lot of things accomplished because of her. But when we broke up I did not feel terribly lonely, because I immediately got in with someone else, but I noticed that the person I went to was kind of crazy like me, so none of us did any class work and I liked that too, but then I failed most of my classes and was kicked out of the college..."

VII. FIRES HAVE TRAITS OF NARCISSISM; NOT ONLY DO THEY NOT MIND OTHER PEOPLE'S ATTENTION, THEY CRAVE IT. THRIVE IN IT.

This is absolutely true. This is yet another reason why nearly all celebrities in our country are fires. People with other elements, especially trees and waters, are usually embarrassed by the public's attention and try to avoid it if they can. But fires are not so. Not only are they fine with the public watching them, they enjoy being the center of everyone's attention, whether it's a secret desire, or reality for them. Fire-people often times dress to attract other people's attention. Fire-people talk so that others can overhear them. Fire-people do crazy things just to be noticed. And they feel just fine walking into a room full of people and having everyone staring at them. They may say, "What are you staring at?" and laugh. Or they may just notice with satisfaction that their new hairstyle and new pair of pants are doing exactly what they wanted them to do. *Fires will dance in public even if they don't know how to dance.* "Dancing, and especially, fast dancing, is one of the cardinal expressions of the Fire element in human culture," wrote Cathy, a fire-girl. "This is why Fires absolutely need to dance with as little clothes on as possible every morning and night." And fires love to sing loudly when they are in public areas as well. Those people who walk or bike by you in the street singing their hearts out are fires.

VIII. FIRE-PEOPLE BREAK OR DESTROY THINGS FAR MORE OFTEN THAN OTHER ELEMENTS.

Just like fire in the natural world can be destructive, people born with fire-Qi break and destroy things easily and they do that often. Here is a testimony written by a mother of a seven year old fire-boy, named Josh; "Learning about 5-elements and understanding that my son has fire energy in him was most helpful. I was beginning to despair because Josh broke all the toys we gave him. He is seven and knows how to close drawers and doors, but he never does. After he uses the bathroom you'd think it was hit by a hurricane. Everything is pulled out of boxes and spread around. The mirror door is wide open and all the rugs are twisted in such a strange way that one wonders how in the world he did it!"

A word of warning for those of you who must share a living space with strong fire types; unless fires study and master the 5-elements they rarely grow out of their destructive streak. Just sit in any restaurant and watch the fully-grown adult fire person drop food on her elegant shirt or the fire executive spill coffee on his new trousers. Even the highly trained fires still break their cars more often than people with other elements. They also wear out their clothes and shoes faster than people with other elements and need repairs in their houses more regularly. In other words, fires burn everything they touch so you may as well get used to it!

IX. FIRES MUST PLAY MORE THAN OTHERS AND LOVE SPORTS.

Fires may appear to other elements as mischievous, unpredictable and always looking for some divertissement kind of people. Because of this we may think them to be less serious and less reliable, especially if we encounter them in the work environment. But in order to fight yawning boredom, a constant threat to the fire personality, they must invent their own games, playing them by themselves or with other people. For example, they may give their coworkers funny nicknames or made-up identities and joke about their colleagues all day long just to amuse themselves. These fire-people are often seen in the corridors fooling around when others remain quietly in front of their computers. Fires are the ones who are usually talking about something "really funny" by a water-fountain or in a copy-room. At a meeting, which was supposed to be very serious, they may do or say something "really funny" just to interrupt the routine, amusing themselves and others. They often make themselves into passionate players of some kind; virtual or real-life basketball, cards, ping-pong, or on-line dating. They can

Fire-people often enjoy competitive sports

play their game, both at work and at home, so much that others around them may get frustrated.

Most athletes are fiery people. They love competition against others and may become very serious about sports. Fire people are known for booing the referee who makes a bad call against their team. Our most famous athletes in sports are usually the ones who can run faster and shoot more accurately than others. This aspect of having speed, agility and strength are all aspects of the fiery personality. Because the fire-person places such a strong value on being physically powerful, they may get depressed when they get older and the body's vitality is not what it once was. Qigong is an excellent way to increase Fire-Qi for people of any age.

X. FIRES LOVE TO EAT AND GET VERY HUNGRY SUDDENLY; IF THEY DON'T EAT RIGHT AWAY THEY CAN BECOME MOODY OR IRRITATED.

Here is a word from a fire-student Mike summarizing this fire-trait perfectly: "I have this thing. I get hungry in the middle of a lecture or in a movie theater, and I really must eat soon, because if I don't I get so moody, I can be mean to any person for no reason at all. My girl-friend Joanne knows about this and she always asks if I have food available. If I say no, she says we must go somewhere and eat. I think my metabolism is so crazy fast that when I don't eat for a while my stomach starts devouring itself. It growls so loudly people around me can hear it, and they look at me with a strange glance as if implying their stomachs never do that. Well, maybe they don't. And even after I've just eaten, I can eat again in half an hour or so. One day I ate dinner three times, my friends were astonished. I think I can do it because I digest food so fast."

Just like natural fire "devours" wood and other fuel in a quick fashion, needing more and more fuel to sustain its flames, the human fires, especially when they are young, can eat larger quantities and more often than people with other elements. Even the more mature fires experience states of hunger in a somewhat dramatic way, which shows they eat their food really fast and still want something after they are done. This is because fires use more energy than other elements due to their constant activities while existing in a constant mode of aggression and persuasion against others.

XI. FIRES LOVE TO TRAVEL. THEY DO IT MORE THAN OTHERS; FIRES WILL TRAVEL AND MOVE OFTEN, REGARDLESS IF THEY CAN AFFORD IT.

Whether it's a bunch of short trips to a desert or a nearby beach, or traveling regularly to far destinations, fires are passionate about escaping their "normal" life. Fire people will go out of their way to get extra vacation days if they can use them for travel. They will travel cheaply, go without hotel accommodations, sleep in cars or in small tents, it does not matter. All they really need is to hit the road and drive away from the life they live every day.

XII. FIRES HAVE HARD TIME BEING ALONE.

In truth, although fires are aggressive or self-assured people, they hate being alone. Its creepy, it's unpleasant, they don't like it. Because of this they find ways to force others into keeping them company and doing something fires themselves want to do but don't want to do alone. In this sense, fires are almost exact opposites of water-people who prefer being alone and feel happily entertained each time

13

they lock the door to their room, diving into the ocean of the cyber-space or self-imagination. Although fires may enjoy reading or writing online as well, they prefer to do it in a café or some other public place where there is a crowd and they are not alone.

XIII. FIRES OFTEN SPEAK IN LOUD VOICES AND HAVE NO PROBLEM INTERRUPTING OTHER PEOPLE WHEN THEY SPEAK.

Fires express themselves powerfully no matter where they are or what they do, unless they are so deprived of their own type of Qi, they can no longer even be a speck of the person they normally are. Healthy fires are almost expected by their friends and enemies to barge into their conversations, or anything else that draws their attention (which is everything) with no consideration whatsoever, about what others think or do. Fires are people who talk very loudly at the table next to you when you are trying to have a quiet romantic dinner in a restaurant. Fires will scream across the entire hall of an airport's waiting area asking their friends to get them a sandwich. Fires scream, cheer and sing loud songs in the shower making the whole house shake with their presence. Just get used to it.

XIV FIRES LOVE SPEED AND DO EVERYTHING VERY QUICKLY. THEY LEARN QUICKLY AND FORGET JUST AS QUICKLY.

Fire person's behavior is marked by high intensity and speed. Everything they do must be done fast. When they are at work this may be a good thing. My fire friend Christy is finished with all her assignments at work while her colleagues are still waiting for more directions to get started. But then the problem is what's next? She is either bored or gets loads more work without being paid extra. Once fires realize the unfairness of this situation, they try to get out of it, but it does not always look pretty.

In my classes, fire students are astounding. They learn things faster than I can say them. The problem is that they will remember nothing by the time we have our next class, because tons of new things have happened to them during that time. The same principle of "burning things fast" applies to each and every aspect of the fire person's life. Food must be served fast. Speed must be maximal when they drive. Getting someone to have sex with them also must take as little time as possible.

XV. FIRES GET ANGRY EASILY AND ARE CAPABLE OF RAGE.

Fires are so aggressive and persistent that they usually get what they want, when they want it. However, when things don't go their way they may become outraged. Fire peoples' anger, especially rage, is a dangerous thing. No one should stand in his or her way. When fires lose mental control entirely they are capable of horrific things. They can do this even to those whom they love. After rage subsides, they try to apologize to the person they hurt, thinking that what they did is not such a big deal (because fires are accustomed to their own state of anger) and everything can return back to normal. However, most who have experienced a fire person's rage will never feel the same way about them.

Fire people have a tendency to become aggressive

XVI. FIRES HESITATE YIELDING TO AUTHORITY NO MATTER HOW FAIR OR POWERFUL IT IS. MANY TRY TO "BEAT THE SYSTEM."

One can easily identify with this if one is a fire person or had a chance to observe a fire person's behavior. Fires often do not respect rules and don't think that there should be any authority over them or other people. Deep in their hearts, fires are natural anarchists.

Because fire-people have strong personalities and can win in most situations involving other people they think the social system is set against them. They think it protects the weak, and they may be right about this. If fires were to be allowed to do what they want, we would be back to medieval fights between knights and the rest of society would be left in ruins. But fires do not see the situation this way. They simply want to be themselves, and they experience real psychological misery when they realize this culture leaves little room for their physical prowess and mental bravery. For this reason, fires sometimes join gangs and other clubs where anti-social behavior is glorified.

Strong fire types often will not work for a system such as a big bank or corporation. They start their own companies, which may be successful or not, depending on whether fires are smart enough to bring metal, tree, earth and water people into their team of executives and honestly share her/his power with them.

XVII. FIRES FORGET THINGS EASILY AND MAY NEED TO BE FREQUENTLY REMINDED OF THEIR PROMISES AND OBLIGATIONS. THEY ALSO HAVE HARD TIME REMEMBERING THEIR PAST.

Despite fires strong mental abilities they have one peculiar weakness; they forget things easily, much faster and more easily than people with other elements do. This is explained by the expansive nature of the fire-person's character. Fires are always on the go, always looking out for something new and exciting. Remembering the past excitement becomes difficult especially when one reaches a certain age. For this reason many smart fires keep journals for the duration of their lives or record audio and video.

XVIII. Fires feel happy around animals. They enjoy playing with children, but only if they do not have a permanent responsibility for their care.

Fires people adore animals. This is because, with animals, they can bring their own animalistic and even beast-like nature to life. When fires are healthy and not oppressed, they love to play wildly, to growl, kick, jump and run fast. They will play with a dog or cat or other creature of nature like a person of another element never could. This is because fires feel they are like animals themselves. Due to the fact our society forces us to be increasingly civilized, meaning we have to suppress our natural urges more for the sake of collective harmony, we tend to lose fiery aspects of our own nature. We become too domesticated, but a fire person can never be fully domesticated. There will always remain some aspect of wild, elemental craziness in their character. Thank God for that! Otherwise humans could become so boring.

When with children, fires play in almost the same manner as they do with animals. In other words they relate to the non-socialized, non-domesticated aspect of a child's personality. Fires do not feel all ecstatic about babies (this is for tree people) but are crazy about toddlers. Fires can spend hours playing with two and three year old little humans who are also happy to play with the fire people. They sense there is no adult inside the adult looking human and it is all fun with no rules or regulations. Yet, fires may ultimately fail as guardians and parents, because the moment they stop having fun with children and the time comes for their grown-up function, boredom settles in and being with a child becomes uninteresting and unexciting. They may easily forget things they have promised the child, because something else distracted their attention. Children may eventually recognize the ultimate selfishness in the fire person's behavior and cool down toward them.

XIX. FIRES SOMETIMES LIKE TO TALK BACK AND ARGUE WITH PEOPLE. THEY CAN EASILY HURT PEOPLE'S FEELINGS AS THEY DO THIS.

Although being blessed with stamina for prolonged debates and arguments is a characteristic of the metal person, fires share with them the desire to have the last word in every conversation they have. Did you ever wonder why teenagers always must say something back at you? This is because, biologically, they are entering the fire-Qi phase, which happens to all of us when we are roughly between twelve and twenty four years old (you read more about the life cycles in chapter six). The difference between teenagers and people with other elements is that the fires will act like this their entire life unless they consciously choose to change. Fire people simply cannot tolerate when another person tells them what to do, and because fires do not listen well to what others are trying to tell them, everything they hear they perceive to be a command of sorts, therefore, they feel they must strike back. Smart parents upon discovering this trait in their children learn to use reverse psychology. When they stop telling their teenagers what they want them to do, they have hopes that it may be accomplished. And if they smartly tell their teens what they "cannot do" it is almost guaranteed that they will try. Believe it or not this works on the fire-adults just as well.

XX. FIRES ABSOLUTELY LOVE THEIR HOT AND SPICY FOODS. THEY CAN BE EASILY HOOKED ON DRUGS, ALCOHOL, AND COFFEE.

Anyone who goes through five to ten cups of coffee or hot tea (or both) every morning is a fire person. Everyone who can drink heavily, and go crazy at a party, rising higher on the power of liquor, is a fire person. Most people who use drugs like speed or uppers to break away from the boredom of our metallic society are fire-people. Fires will try just about anything in these areas. It is good if they choose to try many different types of coffee without getting into trying many different drugs. Fires get hooked on new and exciting substances quickly, but unlike the water-people, they can be unhooked relatively easy.

Chapter Two

Water People

In this chapter, we are going to look at the characteristics of people whose lives are governed by the water element. In general, our society is not very kind to these people. Most of us perceive them as too passive and weak, and we often accuse them of lacking necessary abilities to fight for what they need as well as the ability to defend themselves against other's aggression. Yet, in many other societies, including the native cultures of the Americas and most Asian societies, the water-archetype of human behavior is considered to be the most refined and valuable. These quiet, seemingly withdrawn and philosophically inclined individuals are whom they select as their leaders and cultural heroes.

I. WATER PEOPLE WEAR ALMOST EXCLUSIVELY BLUE, NAVY, GREY AND BLACK COLOR CLOTHES.

When I begin teaching a new class at my university, I quickly glance over my students' clothes. This allows me to identify the water-individuals who I know to be very shy and do not appreciate when I put them on the spot with my provocative questions. These water-students most of the time wear blue jeans and blue hoodies with some kind of grayish, bluish or blackish t-shirt underneath. We may consider this the "water-uniform" which they wear throughout the entire semester, never switching to orange, yellow, red, gold, or bright green colors. Water people are mysteriously drawn to the color of their own element, blue.

They think it is simply the best and while they can tolerate bright-red and orange colors in their environment (because waters can tolerate just about anything), one cannot pay them enough money to make them wear red, orange, or bright-yellow colors on their bodies.

II. WATER-PEOPLE CAN GO TO THE SAME RESTAURANT AND ORDER THE SAME FOOD FOR MANY, MANY YEARS.

Yes, they can! And this is one of their many amazing qualities which most of us like to poke fun at. When you go to a restaurant with your water-friend or water-relative, you don't have to guess what they are going to order. It is going to be the same order over and over again. Waters are stable and predictable people, people who do not like their boats to be rocked. So they figure they need not twist their brains every time they go to a restaurant. This is why they order the same stuff, and always eat what they are used to. When they eat at home it's generally the same meal for breakfast and/or dinner for many, many years. They never seem to grow tired of this monotony until one day, without any comprehensible reason, they switch to another staple they continue to eat for yet another ten years or so.

III. WATERS DO NOT OFTEN SAY "NO" BUT THIS DOES NOT MEAN THEY ARE GOING TO DO WHAT PEOPLE TELL THEM TO DO.

An amazing water behavior that is incomprehensible to other elements, is they rarely give a straightforward "no." This does not mean they are agreeing to something. Water will often withhold their opinions on a situation. If they do give their opinions or answers under pressure, it may be done in such an evasive manner that one is left in doubt as to what they actually meant.

If you ask a water to do something for you or another person, they may or may not do what you requested, but there will be no arguments about it. Fighting them verbally or putting pressure on them in order to accomplish something is useless. They either do what you have asked them to do, or not. While avoiding what you have asked of them, they are polite, pleasant and non-confrontational. It's not as though they rub their disobedience into your face, they just avoid the whole issue altogether. Just how the natural element of water is extremely difficult to compress, using social pressure on water people practically never works. They find a way to avoid unpleasantness without fighting back or explaining why they don't care to. "As a result," one of my water-students said, "we are perceived by other elements as the greatest procrastinators who have ever existed. When in fact all we do is avoid the bullies who always try to take advantage of us, because we never impose our agendas on them".

IV. WATERS ARE INCAPABLE OF THROWING THINGS AWAY, EVEN IF THESE THINGS ARE OLD, BROKEN AND USELESS.

Here is a word from another of my water-students; "I never throw things away. I always think they might still be useful for something, and I can use them one day or someone else will. My mother is fire and she hates it when I stack things around the house and in my room. She has secretly thrown things away thinking I would not notice their disappearance, but I always know when she does. I just don't argue with her because I know it is useless. As fire, she is

Waters are filled with deep meaning and often musical gifts
They are notorious for collecting all manner of things

going to do what she wants to do, and no amount of explaining why it is important for me to keep all my things and collect even more, is going to change her behavior. I learned to keep the possessions that are particularly important to me in secret places, so she won't notice them."

V. STRONG WATER TYPES DISLIKE, AND EVEN FEAR MOVING TO NEW PLACES. EVEN CHANGING FURNITURE AROUND THE ROOM OR HOUSE MAY BE PSYCHOLOGICALLY DIFFICULT FOR THEM.

In nature, water for the most part sits in the same place for a long time, creating ponds, lakes and seas. Water people are most comfortable when they are surrounded by familiar things and stay in the same residence for a long time. Here is a water person's testimony to this; "When I was little, my parents moved all the time because of my father's job. I hated it so much. Every time I would get used to something and begin feeling comfortable in our neighborhood we had to move. I did not do well at school and did not have any friends. What made it worse was my little sister loved it when we moved. She actually looked forward to moving out of our old town. As soon as we arrived in a new place, she would go around announcing that we were moving out in a week or a month and kids must start playing with her right away, because soon we would be gone. I guess this is cause she's fire and I'm water."

VI. WATERS USUALLY REMAIN FRIENDS WITH THE SAME PEOPLE FOR A LONG TIME. IT IS HARD FOR THEM TO MAKE NEW FRIENDS.

This trait is easier to observe in water-people who are in their thirties and forties and still friends with people they

Water people can be slow to make new friends

had known since college or high school. Fires usually go through their relationships very quickly and do not particularly worry about a relationship ending for one reason or another. Waters are very shy and passive in their behavior and it may be extremely difficult for them to initiate a new relationship. For that reason, and also because they can survive through many unpleasant twists and turns of human characters, they usually keep friends for life. This is one of special and most beautiful gifts the water people can give us, to continue being our friend when all other people and even our family have left us.

VII. FEAR IS THE MAIN EMOTION GOVERNING WATER PEOPLE.

Because they are often very quiet and incapable of aggression, internal or external, waters are afraid of many things. They rarely confess this to themselves or to other people and yet, so many decisions in their lives are based on unrecognized (or even recognized) states of fearfulness. Waters will continue working a very bad job because they are afraid that they will never find a new job if they quit the old one. They will continue living in a bad neighborhood simply because moving out of it scares them even more than dealing with bad neighbors. They will endure the unpleasantness of other people's behavior because they are afraid to tell them about it. When a water-person cultivates his character with the knowledge and practice of the 5-elements, this internal inclination toward fear will transform into a great capacity for tolerance and forgiveness. But while in its uncultivated state, fear is the single most hindering factor in the water-person's life.

VIII. WATER PEOPLE PREFER TO STAY AWAY FROM PEOPLE WHO SPEAK IN LOUD VOICES AND TALK A LOT.

Although listening to other people's complaints is one of water person's greatest gifts to other elements, they also have a really hard time listening when others speak in loud voices or talk all the time. If we want to benefit from their natural gift of patience and their supportive way of listening to our complaints about other people, we need to at least learn to speak more quietly, taking breaks between speeches. Otherwise, they simply find a way to avoid listening to us.

IX. WATERS MAY HAVE A LOVE FOR WATCHING HORROR MOVIES.

Jake a former student wrote this comment: "I always enjoyed watching horror movies even when I was a little boy. I always thought everyone liked horror movies until I realized only a particular group of people enjoy them while there are others who never watch them. I also observed that it's the same group of people who love stories of vampires and play lots of video games. When I took Dr. Storch's 5-Elements course I realized this is connected to my being a water person. Since fear is my main emotion I like to connect to people through their fear. In our society people do not express fear and it is punishable to make people scared through cruel pranks. So the only way to connect to my prime emotion is by watching these movies, reading books and playing video games, which are based on fear."

X. Water people feel tired and fatigued more often than other elements.

Because society is ruled by fire and metal elements, the ways of the water people seem strange to most of us. We assume they must adjust to society's norm instead of recognizing the water people's bio-rhythms are different from ours, requiring social accommodations. Our schools and businesses begin operating early in the morning, so water people do not get a chance to follow the internal schedule most beneficial for their health; staying up late and sleeping until noon. This condition alone is enough to alter and even destroy the natural rhythms of their bodies and minds. Being tired may become a constant presence in their life. Additionally, water people's bio-magnetic fields are regularly "boiled" by the fires' hyperactive behavior. Most of us who are fires and metals speak too loudly and too much and act too aggressively for water peoples taste.

XI. Waters are often bored by People of other elements, especially by Fires.

You probably understand why the fire-personality is constantly bored and needs more entertainment all the time. But can you understand that the waters are also bored by other people?! They are, but for a distinct reason and it's expressed in a different manner. Waters are bored by the fire and metal people, because from the water's position, they have nothing to say. Most of the usual talk which fire and metal people find entertaining does not appeal to the waters.

Waters are more observant than other elements, so they already know ahead of time what most of us are going to say to them and to each other. They also have no interest in the information that could be helpful for domination over people. "This is what fire-metal people talk about," said one of my students. "If we take personal domination topics out of the conversation, fire and metal people actually have little to say to each other." This of course is of little interest to the water person.

Waters are more inclined to have conversations of a spiritual or philosophical nature. They likely do not care which team wins the superbowl or what kind of car you drive.

To avoid personal domination based conversations, waters create their own circles of interest, which other elements like to call "geek and weirdo circles." Here they are free to do what they really enjoy, playing their own games, effectively shutting down the outside world. The Internet, or the Cyber-Ocean, is a creation of the water-persons' genius. They can be active in a non-physical way and their shy personalities can grab the attention of the entire world.

XII. WATER PEOPLE REMAIN COOL-COMPOSED IN THE MIDDLE OF VERY UNPLEASANT MOMENTS, SUCH AS A HEATED DEBATE AMONG FRIENDS OR FISTFIGHT IN A BAR.

Under certain situations things may be completely out of control, yet the water-person will be directly in the middle of the conflict and outside of it at the same time. Their facial expression won't even change despite the surrounding madness. A water person won't show emotions one way or another while he quietly walks away from screaming, fighting people. Or he may choose to stay, filled with strange curiosity mixed with responsibility, until people are done screaming and fighting with each other. Then he will attend to other's wounds inflicted from battle.

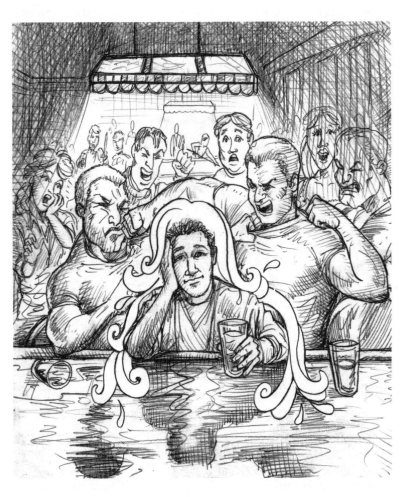

Water people are known for avoiding drama

This behavior may surprise (even water people themselves), because they are not known as courageous people. Yet, within a serious conflict they often play an important role. It's as if there is a simple shift with the addition of a quiet, non-violent person in the middle of a conflict. If they choose to waters can be the best inborn peace-makers. Making peace by simply being present during conflict, they judge no one, take no one's side, and wait for the fight to end, where they offer to wash away other's pain.

XIII. WATER PEOPLE OFTEN KEEP COLLECTIONS SUCH AS; BOTTLES, MATCH-BOXES, RECORDS, CDs, BOOKS, STATUES, POSTERS OR ANYTHING WHICH THEY ARE VERY ATTACHED TO.

Not only do water people never throw anything away, they constantly bring more new things into the house. When I say "new" this is not necessarily literally new, just that it wasn't in house before. An item could be thrown away by one person and rescued by the water person. Those of us, (like me) who are married to a water person, know the struggle to get rid of hundreds of useless objects found in every closet and drawer of the house we share. Despite my very effective fight against the multiplication of objects in our house, my watery partner always wins. The day after I cleaned and emptied a closet I found a half-broken vacuum-cleaner. When I approached my water-husband, he said he would fix it. "But we already have three vacuum cleaners that don't work!" I exclaimed. He coolly replied, "I will fix one of them. When it breaks I will fix another, and then another." The reality was it never came to this and I discretely threw away yet another object that didn't work into a garbage bin.

Waters also love to collect things of particular categories, beads, animal statues, sports cards, whatever resonates with their secret fantasy-world. Unlike the metal-element collectors, water people do not remember how many collected items they have. Because they do not follow a particular design-classification while collecting, they always have hard time finding what they want (when they want it) amongst their multiple collections.

Additionally waters are known for their strange fondness of boxes, which can reach mythological proportions in some. A water person who lives in the same residence for many years will probably have hundreds of different style boxes around the house, some of which are used while others aren't. And of course waters are strongly possessive of all their belongings, including the boxes, disliking when people touch or throw them away.

XIV. WATER PEOPLE MAY HAVE A HARD TIME TALKING TO, OR IN THE PRESENCE OF PEOPLE THEY DO NOT KNOW.

Waters are often extremely shy, secretive people. They suffer a lot from other peoples' aggressive elements, mainly fire and metal. This is why they prefer to stay in the shady areas during all human communications. They try to avoid expressing their opinions publicly as much as possible, even when they have been specifically asked for it. They do so because they either do not know what their opinion really is or are afraid that expressing it might cause some unpleasant situation. Kim, one of my water students explained, "When people ask me what I think about something it is always a struggle for me. First, I am aware that when people ask about something they are actually searching for some kind of support or approval of their position and I do not like that. I do not like to support anyone's positions. Another reason I don't like to share my views is that people always distort what I say. Except for my closest friend, who is water like me, I cannot really talk to anyone. People do not listen. They talk to themselves. So, why to bother? But of course, in the end, my reputation suffers. Most of my other friends think that I simply not smart enough to have an opinion about something. But I ignore them."

XV. WHILE WATERS ARE USUALLY VERY OBSERVANT OF "OTHER PEOPLE'S BEHAVIOR" THEY HAVE A HARD TIME UNDERSTANDING THEMSELVES OR WHAT THEY REALLY WANT.

Waters are usually the wisest individuals and in a group they know other people's weaknesses and strengths better than they themselves know. However, when it comes to understanding themselves waters are less capable than those with other elements. *It is easy for water to reflect images of all things, but extremely challenging for water to reflect upon itself.* This particular trait adds to the waters' passive ways in life. If they don't know what they want... how can they be propelled into action?

One water student said, "In all the years of my life, somebody else made all the important decisions for me. It was someone else who decided where I would live and what job I would take. Although I was not particularly happy with the decisions my parents and then my wife were making for me, I understood that this is how it was going to be, because I was without a desire to make decisions of my own. All my efforts were then concentrated on adjusting to a situation where I found myself, and I realized that, actually, it works just fine. My wife takes care of all our moving and finding home arrangements. Then she forces me to get a job, and then I just maintain the status quo. As long as she is somehow content with what I do for her and for my family I am free to live in the world of my fantasies. I play videogames when she is fast asleep and record music when she is cleaning or cooking. When she specifically asks for help I always provide it, but I am never around just for the sake of keeping or needing the company of others."

XVI. WATER PEOPLE SOMETIMES DON'T LIKE DRINKS AND FOODS THAT ARE HOT IN TEMPERATURE.

I can easily identify people with innate Qi of water by offering them drinks and food hot in temperature. Just like smart animals don't eat food that is too hot, the water people will not eat their food or drink their tea until they become cooler, almost room temperature. Then they will enjoy them. I know that this is a very healthy habit and I am constantly reminded about that by my new friend, Chinese doctor and Acupuncturist, Susan Wang, who never drinks tea that is too hot and lets her food cool down for a few minutes before she eats. My innate energy is that of fire and thus I more enjoy foods served warm or hot. On the contrary, waters often don't like overly hot foods, preferring raw salads, fruits etc.

XVII. WATER PEOPLE CAN REMAIN IN A DIFFICULT SITUATION WITHOUT COMPLAINING OR DOING SOMETHING ABOUT IT.

Indeed Water people, have a remarkable ability to stay in the same place, job or relationship for a very long time, doing nothing to change their situation even if they do not particularly enjoy it. For instance, a water person can remain in a relationship with a partner even if they know that the partner is not faithful to them. As long as some status quo is reached and water is not forced into any pressure to change the situation, the water can cope with the deceit, not even asking any questions.

Because it takes so much of their energy to adapt to life situations, which are constantly created and changed by other people around them, water personalities are very attached to the memories of their past such as their old houses, family, school, friends, and so forth. In this respect they are opposites of the fire people who move through life quickly, constantly creating new conditions and new relationships, too many to remember all of them! Although waters remember their past well they may have memory problems with the more immediate things, like what they wished to say to someone during a meeting.

XVIII. WATER PEOPLE ARE OFTEN SECRETIVE AND ARE CAPABLE OF KEEPING SECRETS, THEIR OWN AND OTHER'S, FOR A LONG TIME.

Often times water people do not fight for what they need, but this does not mean they are without needs of their own. They have just an active imagination as fires, but express their curiosities and fantasies differently. Waters like to exist in a world where either no one or only selected few can participate. Of course the modern invention of video-games is a revenge the water energy is taking on all of us. With their strong fantasies of a world distinctive from the one previous generations created, water-people are free to live in a completely different world as soon as they turn on the switch of their computer or game-station.

In terms of their private lives, waters exist in a secretive, imaginary world. Anything that requires heavy lifting in terms of personal social expression, does not appeal to them. Just like their native element water people endowed with this mysterious energy prefer to lie low, reflecting the images cast by other people's lives, like the surface of the lake, and not get involved. This certainly provides for a withdrawn and secretive personality, as we all know them to have. On the positive end is the fact that waters are able to keep any secret you share with them. While a person with any other element (especially fire) may immediately tell everyone what you just asked to never mention. On the negative side, waters usually hide their love affections and other serious psychological needs and desires so deeply we may never find out about them until they die and we read their diary, or until they let us into their chamber of secrets.

XIX. WATERS HAVE VIVID DREAMS REGULARLY

Water-people and those with strong water element usually feel they must sleep a lot and while they do, their dreaming is very active. Upon awakening it is hard for them to separate dreams from real life. Many of their dreams are both vivid and sometimes unpleasant -- as if they took it upon themselves the difficult job of clearing other people's nightmares. This characteristic of the water's behaviors is related to what I describe in the next point as "active kidneys function" during the night hours. *Waters are typically physically passive during daytime hours* (if they must move a lot due to their employment they do it in an autopilot state) and yet their mind continues to be very active and observant of many different things. As their rich impressions and perceptions may not find a sufficient exit during the day, night time becomes the only opportunity for their consciousness to deal with the information gathered. If waters become more mentally present during the day hours and especially if they physically exercise before they go to sleep they will have an easier and more pleasant dreaming experience. The water people are the main night dreamers.

XX. WATER PEOPLE HAVE A HABIT OF HOLDING THE NEED TO USE THE BATHROOM UNTIL IT IS ALMOST TOO LATE.

They sometimes have a hard time asking permission to use the bathroom when they are in other people's homes. When staying in hotels it may be a big problem to go "number two" according to usual schedule. Water people often had the childhood habit of wetting the bed at night. These forms of behavior are due to the fact that the water people's kidney world is over stimulated. They like to stay up late and they enjoy their late evening or even mid-night meal as their best meal because they rarely feel real pangs of hunger during the earlier hours of the day. The price for this habit is taking solid and liquid waste out of the body becomes a difficult procedure at night. One of my water friends explains, "I am so lucky that my girlfriend is a tree person and very compassionate woman. She understands that I must be very slow in the morning and that it may take a long time until I am ready to go to the bathroom. She sometimes laughs at me, but in a friendly kind of way. She gets up early and is done with her toilet routine even before I can wake up."

Chapter Three

Tree People

The Tree people are the ones we usually take advantage of because they seem to have an endless amount of sweetness and kindness in their character, as well as the natural ability to sacrifice their own interests for the sake of others. We other elements often rely on the vital force of the tree people for our very survival or for having a good time. We rarely realize how much it costs them energetically to support us. We rarely thank them for their sacrifices, and even if we do it may still be not enough to replenish what we have taken. This is why one of the first characteristics of the tree-personality involves the following.

I. TREE-PEOPLE ENJOY EATING FOODS WITH SWEET TASTE SUCH AS; CHOCOLATE, CANDIES, CAKES, AND ICE CREAM. THEY MIGHT FEEL THEY HAVE TO EAT SWEETS REGULARLY.

Indeed it is easy to know who is a Tree-person in your circle of relatives and friends, and who is not. All you have to do is regularly inspect their refrigerator and look at what sits on top of their kitchen counters. If the frozen food section regularly contains a jar or two of ice-cream we are in the presence of a tree person. If one day you look and the ice-cream isn't there, it's probably because it was eaten in its entirety last night over a sad and depressing movie or right after a conversation with a friend who complained about another friend. There will be plenty of chocolate bars and cookies in the house. There will be fruit bars and fresh fruit,

Tree people are known for craving sweets

as well as dry fruit and canned fruit. And there will be a cake or a dream of eating it! The tree people know that eating all this sugar is not good for them, and yet adding sweetness to everything they eat makes them feel so much better that they cannot resist! A tree-person, Monica expressed her relationship with sugar in this way: "I am very much into exercises and spiritual stuff. I do yoga and I have been a vegetarian for ten years. I drink my own water and I never crave anything unhealthy, except for sugar. Sugar is my passion and my worst enemy. I know it is not good for me, but every time I come home from work and am upset about something I find myself eating something sweet like a Danish, or a cookie or ice cream. And I don't even know how this happens, I mean, it must be a totally unconscious life-restoring behavior because I can fight off any addiction, but not sugar. *It was only after I realized that I'm a tree-person and want everything to taste sweet, I began switching from sweet foods to sweet actions.* When I get to hear sweet words from my friends I crave less sugar, so I decided to record my own voice saying something nice about myself. I am now playing my positive affirmations in the morning before I have breakfast and in the afternoon, as soon as I come home from work, and I have noticed a difference. If I remember to play the tape before breakfast I can go without sugar until lunch."

II. TREE-PEOPLE CRY OFTEN. THEY MAY CRY SEVERAL TIMES A WEEK AND WHEN THEY DO THEIR TEARS COME OUT EASILY.

They might sit in a movie theater watching a scene where an animal is about to be hurt and start sobbing uncontrollably. People look at them thinking, "What's wrong with you? Why are you such a cry-baby?" But a tree-person cannot help the tears. Male trees more likely know how to hide their teary eyes, because they have been teased and even tortured so many times in their lives due to their tears, it simply is not worth it to cry publicly. However, at home when no one sees them, they cry liberally and like the feeling. Female trees have an easier time with public crying, but still feel embarrassed by it quite regularly because they don't know when it is going to happen and because they don't want other people to think it's such a big deal.

People dominating with elements other than tree, do not cry so often and this is why it is such a big deal for them. *Metal people practically never cry.* If someone made a metal person cry they will remember it forever. When metals are turned to tears it ruins everything for them. They must be terribly hurt to let tears roll in front of another person. *This is why metals cannot stand it when trees cry in their company.* They honestly think this must be the end of the world for someone who is crying like this, but for the trees it is not the end of the world. *For them, it is normal!*

Fires do not go into tears often, because the fire person's response to pain is anger or even rage. This usually takes care of their need to cry, because someone else will have to cry instead. And waters are too calm to become so deeply disturbed that they cannot wait to cry at another time. Since Earth people usually feel OK about most things in life, they too live without a need to express themselves through tears. This leaves the tree-people in a unique position, because they do experience a deep seated need to respond personally and emotionally to all the injustices ever done to them, as well as to other people, animals, and plants. If they feel sorry for them they must cry.

A tree-person Michelle says: "I carry a small box of tissues in my purse, because I never know when I am going to cry making my make-up melt. But I do cry all the time.

And it's not because I am an unhappy person, I am just so easily moved by so many things, especially when someone is hurt or tells the story of how badly they had been treated. I know I am going to cry when something like this happens. I don't understand why other people are so heartless or why they hide their feelings so they never cry. Don't they feel the same way I do?"

III. TREE PEOPLE ARE EXCEEDINGLY KIND TO OTHERS, ALMOST TO A FAULT, BUT SOME TREES KNOW HOW TO CHANGE IT.

Their kindness is legendary. But may be irritating to a metal person whose life is based on following a schedule, not on spontaneous acts of kindness designed to help those who are in need. Whether we applaud trees for their heroic efforts in saving others or scold them for being late, depends on where you are in relation to a particular Tree-person. My husband is water and tree. Water is difficult to deal with when we are arranging a date or vacation, but it is the function of the tree energy in my husband's behavior that can actually drive me mad. One time he was three hours late for a special date, because he was helping the parents of a woman who worked in his office four years prior. I mean, he barely knew that woman. He never met her parents. And it was supposed to be our fun-and-play day, a rare opportunity for us, because he works so hard and yet, he stayed there for three hours fixing their toilet and did not even call me, because he felt uncomfortable asking their permission to use their telephone to call his wife! This I think describes the degree to which the tree person is willing to sacrifice his own happiness for the sake of other people's comfort. But it does not have to be that way!

During my long life, I have met a good number of tree people who have learned the true power of kindness begins by developing kindness toward oneself. We are not talking about egoistic behavior here. It's simply that truly strong tree people take good care of themselves. As they avoid causing harm to other people they also avoid causing harm to their own personal emotional, physical and mental aspects. It takes a while to learn this practice, but worth the time and effort. No one can show as much sweet and natural kindness toward other people and be as persistent and strong in the non-violent ways of persuasion and disciplining as the Tree people.

When we are in trouble, especially deep emotional trouble, we intuitively reach out for a tree person in our circle of friends. We call them on the phone or try to sit with them to talk our hearts out. *The Tree will stay with us for an hour or longer depending on our need, listening to our disturbing stories told in a voice saturated with toxic negativity.* After they make us feel better, the tree person may start feeling really bad if they are not accustomed to practicing kindness toward themselves. Mostly due to their naturally developed empathy, tree people tend to take other people's pain upon themselves, almost like Jesus did when he died on the cross for our sins. But remember, He was God and his resources were unlimited. You are a human and even when you rely on a divine connection with God your resources are still small compared to how much pain is here on the planet!

If you are a tree you may have noticed this pattern; After taking care of someone else's problem you suddenly realize you no longer have energy to go on with original visions you had for the day, you are not practicing kindness toward yourself, and therefore, your kindness toward others will not last. At some point, you will snap and begin hating others' constant needs for your help without reciprocal behavior in return. Remember you are a tree and you can always grow enough kindness to feed your own heart with the love you so strongly deserve.

IV. TREES GREATLY ENJOY EVERYTHING ROMANTIC: SONGS, BOOKS AND MOVIES EVERYTHING ABOUT LOVE FEEDS THEIR SOUL.

Trees loose their vital force easily, but can retrieve it just as effortlessly. Their internal Qi movement can be compared to that of a plant. You see a plant with withered leaves in the evening, you give it a little water and fertilizer, and in the morning, its leaves turn a shiny healthy-green. There is even a little bloom sticking shyly out from under a leaf. What works a similar type of magic for tree persons are encounters with beautiful, kind, loving and romantic things, especially when they unfold right in front of their eyes (either imagined or real). They usually have a book or two which they are compelled to read over and over again, or a movie they have watched a dozen times or more. This is because the book or movie expresses a particular view of life that perfectly fits the Tree-person's vision or fantasy. Even if there is some sadness there, it is usually a kind and forgiving way of seeing the world. It allows the Tree to see her or his idealized universe as real, and it does not matter that it exists only in a book, movie or song. What matters is that it is sweet, filled with love, nurturing the tree's energy and ability to give love to others.

V. Close to nature, Tree people love to take care of plants, children & animals.

It only makes sense that tree people are the best gardeners among us. Plants in the houses and backyards of people with too much metal or too much fire usually die very quickly. But plants taken care of by a tree person thrive even in difficult climate conditions. It's their magic and nothing can be done about it!

Trees are also most loved by animals and little children. All living beings who depend directly on the supply of unconditional love for their survival respond to trees in a most positive way. You may say they are drawn to tree people in mysterious and unexplainable ways. If you wish to decide whether your boy-friend or girl-friend have the Tree energy, take them somewhere where there will be little children or pet animals. If children and pets go immediately to your friend and freely interact with them showing no fear, your friend has tree energy. If a child, dog, or cat avoid the person you brought, or begin acting strangely around them, your friend has very little or no tree-energy. It does not mean of course, that tree-deficient people are bad or that they should not take care of pets or become parents, because they will surely show appreciation for pets and children in a way that is different from that of a tree personality.

Tree people love to nurture plants and grow organic food

VI. Tree people sympathize with the defeated, not with the victorious. They take the side of the injured, not the one who caused it.

Tree people always feel the pain of the victim. If the victim turns his or her luck around, becoming victorious to the point of punishing or persecuting another person, the tree will withdraw their emotional support. The trees sympathize with the defeated, and this safeguards them against becoming aggressors and persecutors themselves. One particular area of life where this trait shows up regularly is tree peoples' unconscious resistance to climbing the career-ladder. To them becoming top-executive is associated with abusing people, aggressiveness and being unfair.

Tree people may also believe they do not deserve the good things in life because so many people on this planet are miserable. So the trees unconsciously believe they are responsible and therefore must suffer. They feel they must punish themselves for allowing the suffering of others to exist. *For these reasons we rarely find a tree-person in charge of a big bank or corporation or in high positions in judiciary and justice fields.* Trees are always looking for ways to help others and they feel they must do that without assuming responsibilities that require judging people.

VII. Tree people may not be good at fighting for their own interests, but their strength grows a lot when they have to protect other people.

I believe Maya, a tree student of mine, said it best; "When I am under attack of any kind I never have the strength or desire to protect myself. I usually start feeling sorry for the person who tries to verbally attack me or do something negative to me. I think to myself, maybe this person was abused as a child, or maybe they are having a really bad day. But when someone attacks my friends something changes in me. My friends noticed that all of a sudden, I begin defending my friends. I start arguing with people who attack them and I can actually say things that are not in my nature to say, simply because I feel so strongly that I must protect my loved ones. When I am defending my friends I sometimes feel I stop caring about everything else and I usually regret it later. I often apologize to people who I have spoken to in a harsh way. I guess this is how the tree people are. When we have to do something for ourselves we are not as motivated, but we are quick to sacrifice ourselves for the sake of our loved ones."

VIII. Trees are easily hurt by others uncaring words, display of indifference and overall lack of appreciation.

In short, when we are dealing with the Tree energy we are dealing with very sensitive people. Just like a big tree can be taken down by a chainsaw in matter of minutes, a tree-person can be hurt by a short exchange of words or glances. Because tree people always go out of their way to be nice to other people, they simply don't understand that someone's indifference or ill-aimed humor does not mean they hate them. This is a normal thing for them! But remember, we measure others by the experiences we have through our own elements. If a female tree-person believes that only to a very bad person will someone say such a thing and if it's now been said to her, this makes her a very bad person. You get the picture. She will most likely begin to cry. Or if the tree person is a male, he will become anxious, defiant and unable to proceed with the original plan. Trees are sensitive to vulgar words, dirty looks, everything that is impure and not nice in intention unless, out of self-defense, they have developed a degree of tolerance to such things. Yet no amount of tolerance can make a tree person as unemotional and resilient against the unpleasantness of other people as metal people naturally are.

Even when the trees realize how vulnerable they ar because of their natural inclination toward being easily hurt, they still chose to live their lives through emotions. It is unthinkable for them to stop connecting to the world through their feelings just for the sake of their safety. In rare cases, trees become metals, but I will discuss that in chapter seven.

IX. TREES OFTEN HAVE LOTS OF DOUBTS ABOUT THEMSELVES AND ARE NOT SURE IF THEY'RE DOING THE "RIGHT THING."

They may be said to be the most worrying people of all the elements. Like trees in a natural world whose branches are always swaying in the wind, *the tree-people's minds are in constant chatter, where good ideas and concerns about helping others are mixed with fears and thoughts created by lack of self-confidence.* Here are just a few examples shared with me by trees in my seminars: "Is it the right thing to call and tell her that her boyfriend is cheating on her?" Or; "Should I buy him a gift for his birthday or will he think that I'm hitting on him? But I am not hitting on him! I just feel for him because he is lonely." Or; "Should I tell the professor that three students broke into her computer and got the correct answers and this is why they got A+'s when everybody else failed? Should I say this or is it going to make things worse?" Or; "What is my family going to think of me if I get a job as a belly dancer? Are they likely to get angry that I am becoming some sort of a prostitute? But I like to dance and I need money! Oh, what am I going to do?!" Even when a decision has been already made, trees naturally continue doubting and worrying.

Tree can drive their metal or fire partners nuts and can irritate even their water partners by asking so many questions intended to find out whether they are doing the right thing, or not. But since judging and comparing are some of the most difficult things for the tree element, how can they even know what is right and what is wrong? Wrong for what? Or right for whom?

To deal with this problem, some trees learn metallic skills that allow them to more clearly define their life goals and better ways to accomplish them. Others connect to God by praying for guidance, visions and answers to their questions. But so many tree people seem to constantly abide in this state of uncertainty and confusion.

Those tree people who are prohibited to verbally express their doubts and feelings of uncertainty (such as young children or wives of very metallic husbands) learn to avoid voicing their internal torments. Yet, just by looking at them, one can tell what they are suffering from. Their faces are ridden with anxiety. Whether they remain silent or say something their faces turn red, because they are so unsure of themselves. They will also do lots of hand waving and most likely be touching their hair or something else around their head as if indicating great difficulty in thinking straight.

X. TREE PEOPLE MAY HAVE DIFFICULTY WITH FINANCES AND CAN STRUGGLE WITH MONEY, YET, THEY SOMETIMES HAVE VISIONARY IDEAS IN BUSINESS WORTH BILLIONS OF DOLLARS.

This is almost a mystery to me. No matter how small the metal person's income is, they always find a way to gain control over their financial situation. Trees are the exact opposite. No matter how much money they make, their spending usually exceeds the income. In terms of elemental power explanation is easy; strong tree-personalities have very little metal energy in them, and money in essence is metal. However, money is not everything, and as time goes on more people realize no amount of money can save the world from the ecological disaster fast approaching. In this respect, it is the tree energy that is able to "think ecologically in an interconnected way" while metals' thinking may be limited by considerations of immediate financial gains. Tree-energy engineers and business entrepreneurs come with visions that excite thousands of people, and it is through this excitement and great personal fulfillment that their projects become successful. To see a balance of metal and tree in business, one does not need to go any further than the Supreme Science Qigong Foundation. They are a successful organization with a 4-day natural healing seminar for $99. It is a business-savvy organization, yet it gives everyone who wants the knowledge the ability to afford it.

There are thousands of such tree-energy based businesses in this country alone with many more thousands around the globe. It is possible that soon our consciousness will rise to a level of understanding whereby we realize that if a product is hurting the environment or other people it simply is not worth buying or investing in.

XI. TREES CAN HAVE MESSY ROOMS AND HOUSES, BUT ONE CAN FEEL WELCOME THERE.

When you enter the forest you don't expect things to be clean and orderly. Forest is messy and so is a tree person's residence. There is a difference between how the water person's house can become disordered compared to the messiness of a tree's. Water person's dwelling may feel so abandoned, withdrawn and dark inside you may think no one lives there. The tree-person's house is not so dark and withdrawn, but it is messy. The house may have pets, pet smells (complete with pet dirt here and there) plants, and plenty of unfinished projects lying around, as well as objects of beauty, books and boxes of food. All this stuff will appear disorganized, and for a true metal person like myself, this would seem like a disaster. But this is not so at all for people with water, earth, fire or tree elements. In fact they may feel more relieved in the tree person's house, because they don't have to worry about messing things up as they do when they are visiting the impeccably ordered residences of the metallic people.

The tree people know their houses are messy and they wish to make them cleaner as this would help them develop some of the metal energy in their character. Yet, it is difficult for them to find time to do it. Trees are always busy taking care of other people's lives so they don't have enough time or energy to take care of their own needs.

Some trees learn how to strengthen their character by showing kindness toward themselves and create houses that become everyone's dream. These houses are not based on cleanliness or symmetry, but on the principles of "Feng Shui". Feng Shui is the natural flow of energy using specific placements of furniture, flower arrangements, mirrors, water fountains, and other items that enhance Qi.

XII. TREES OFTEN BECOME VEGETARIANS OUT OF COMPASSION.

Today many people consider eating a vegetarian diet for various reasons. It can be religious, protection of the environment or something else. All tree people who I spoke to became vegetarians because they cannot stand the idea of hurting another being for food. Here is a word from Nick: "I became a vegetarian when I was a little boy. We lived on a farm and when I realized where my parents take meat from I could not eat it. My mom and especially my dad were outraged because meat-eating was such a big thing on the farm, but I prevailed. I was not a strong boy, I remember that my brothers could easily gain upon me, but no one could make me eat the dead animal's body. When it was time to slaughter one of our animals I would run away and hide so as not hear or see anything and I would feel bad after they had killed the animal for many days. My dad tried to change me by giving me nothing to eat except meat and I was able to resist. Today I am what my girl-friend calls "a gentle giant." I eat only bread, fruit and vegetables and even though I grew up to be a big fellow I cannot hurt anyone, not a human, not an animal, not even a plant."

XIII. TREES CANNOT STAND ARGUING WITH OR BE PRESENT WHEN OTHERS ARGUE.

In the next chapter, when we examine the metal person's characteristics, we will learn that metal people are fond of debates and arguments. Trees are the opposite of metal as they cannot stand debates and arguments. They may say something contrary just so they can escape doing what they think is a bad idea, but they will not enjoy a prolonged and intense debate intended to defeat or support a certain proposition. Therefore we may unfortunately think of the tree people as not being particularly smart, or we may not find it interesting to talk to them because of their tendency to politely agree with us on every point. Our culture is very metallic in nature. We love a good contrast and we need it to measure things up to understand them better. Even beautiful classical music is based on counterpoints. However, trees feel that every time people debate, there is potential for disagreement. They also know in their hearts that if people disagree with each other, someone may take offense eventually becoming enemies with those they are in disagreement with. Therefore, in most debates trees feel the potential for war, and they absolutely cannot stand it when people hurt each other.

XIV. TREES SOMETIMES USE LIES AS A WAY OF BEING NICE TO OTHER PEOPLE AND THEY ARE NOT PARTICULARLY GOOD AT THAT.

I would say this is a unique characteristic of the tree personality. All of us lie occasionally with various degrees of success. Yet, the tree people are so absolutely terrible at lying that everyone, even children can see through it. It is a little bit ironic, because trees may find themselves using lies more often than other people and still they do not become the masterful liars fire people can naturally be. So, what is happening here?

Trees lie mainly so they can be nice to other people or avoid hurting them. A water-person will find ways to say nothing, a fire-person says whatever comes to her or his mind, and a metal-person will try to act as someone who is always right, but the tree-person will try to come up with something they think is good for another person. Their intention is unmistakably good, yet because the trees say so many little and seemingly innocent lies, they constantly get into trouble because of it. Often they do not remember the lie they said to a person a day before when delivering a new batch of sweet and not-entirely true words. She or he says for example, "Well, it's OK that you broke up with your boy-friend because you know you deserve so much better..." But her friend explodes in return: "But yesterday you said you were sure he still loves me, so which one is true?"

As a result, those of us who are not tree element stop listening to the tree people's nice, sweet commentaries and suggestions, dismissing them all as just wishful thinking. But it would be a big mistake to do so.

XV. TREES OFTEN FEEL A STRONG DESIRE TO WITHDRAW OR RUN AWAY FROM EVERYONE, EVEN PEOPLE THEY LOVE SO MUCH.

Once again all of us regardless of what element we are may occasionally feel we have reached the end of our rope trying our best in a certain situation, and will feel it is time to let go off everything to recharge our batteries. But this is not what I am talking about. This particular state of despair mixed with sadness and complete physical and psychological exhaustion is unique to the tree personality, because they are trying harder than anyone else to be nice and kind to other people while other people, simply because their thoughts and actions are governed by other elements, do not see their kindness or do not appreciate it.

The life of a tree person in our society is a little bit like the life of a tree in our neighborhood. It is there, it gives us shade, makes the air cleaner, it hosts the singing birds and makes the street looking more beautiful. Yet, if the tree drops too many leaves on an expensively renovated roof people will cut the tree down, without suffering any sleepless nights over the matter either.

The same happens in the life of a tree person every day. Here is a word from my tree friend, Jimmie; "I am just too kind for this society. When I come with an offer of help, people do not feel thankful, they feel suspicious. I can read it in their minds; "And what do you want from me, freak? Because surely you are not offering for me to stay in your house for a month for nothing! You want something in return and this is creepy."

Many tree students report that people's responses to their offers to help drove them to tears, because they were called weirdoes, perverts or other bad names simply because they were offering real help to other students stuck in unfortunate situations. Many more students with tree energy reported that other students use them when they need their help, but do not think much about it. When they organize parties or go out for dinner they invite other, more popular and more exciting kids while trees stay at home uninvited.

XVI. Tree people are very forgiving this tempts people governed by other elements to take advantage.

Tree people have a hard time holding a grudge against someone who has wronged them. It is more costly for them psychologically, to feel bad about someone than to let the whole thing go and act as if nothing has happened. *This is perhaps the single greatest strength of tree people!*

When I train my tree students, helping them to become more assertive and self-fulfilled members of our communities, I always tell them there is a difference between forgiving someone and acting as if nothing happened. While all other elements (except maybe earth people who are somewhat similar to trees in this respect) understand what I am talking about, tree people do not. It takes them a long time to realize what that difference might be and it takes them even longer to learn how to practice this realization in their daily behavior.

Here is a story illustrating this point; Natalie, a tree person, has a mother and a sister. Her sister Rachel is both metal and water elements. Rachel has being using her mother's resources; money, land, property, cars, etc., to support herself, her husband and her child, while keeping Natalie out of receiving an equal share of financial support. Rachel's rationale for receiving more than Natalie has always been; "I am a mother and I have given the very first grandson to our family, making our mother very happy. Therefore, I deserve all this support. Natalie is single and can always earn enough money for herself. If Natalie does not earn enough money for herself it is because she is lazy, and why should we reward her for that?"

Before taking my 5-Elements class, Natalie always forgave her "evil" sister and continued to behave as if nothing happened. She did not wish to upset her mother and she truly wanted to be allowed to play with Rachel's son, Nick whom she absolutely adored. After learning about the 5-elements Natalie realized that forgiving Rachel does not mean she must submit herself to her intrigues for as long as Rachel was willing to use them. So instead she cultivated her own metal and water skills, and talked to her mother explaining that she deserves equal respect to her sister regardless of whether or not she is married or has children. She also told her mother she understood she may wish to give Rachel more, but that she thought this was unfair.

Natalie also decided that she was no longer willing to participate in family events during which Rachel mocked her for being childless, for not being able to find a husband and for making so little money. Natalie announced this to her whole family with a broad smile coming from a place of forgiveness and love, but her words were delivered with self-respect and determination. Things began to change. Natalie's mother realized how unjust her distribution of wealth had being and began to support Natalie. She also started seeking Natalie's company alone, without Rachel or her grandchild being around. And this was the beginning of a new life for Natalie.

XVII. TREES HAVE A STRONG SENSE OF SMELL. TURNED OFF BY UNPLEASANT SMELLS, THEY ARE EMPOWERED BY PLEASANT SMELLS, ESPECIALLY FROM INCENSE AND ESSENTIAL OILS.

I dare to say that nearly all people who work with aromatherapy are tree energy or have a sufficient amount of this element in their character. Essential oils as well as all pleasantly aromatic smells such as flowers, candles or cookies often accompany the tree people's lives as though

Trees love to make their body and house smell magical

they have intuitively found a representation of their own element in human society.

Tree people are extremely good at growing flowers and learn quickly about the healing properties of essential oils. When trees are exposed to unpleasant smells, no matter how imperceptible to other elements, they end up with strong headaches, and if they are exposed to these smells for a long time they develop allergies and sinusitis. One can immediately recognize a tree person when he or she walks into a house saying, "Oh, it smells so good in here..." A good smell is a signal for a tree person that the environment they are about to enter is safe. At the same time, upon entering an environment where the tree energy might be hurt, they may suddenly begin complaining about a weird or unpleasant smell which a member of a different element cannot catch.

When trees are talking about their scent experiences we often think they are making things up or that they are too gentle and must stop being so sensitive to their environments. However, it is important to understand; Trees *are not making up their smelling sensations,* they really have them. They cannot stop being sensitive, this is who they are! So people with other elements, especially metal and fire elements, try to remember trees *can* smell what you *cannot*. If you force them to remain in a place where their sensitive nature is not happy you will deal with a dysfunctional, sick tree-person as a result. Strange, incurable stomach conditions, allergies and migraines are just a few things your loved one will develop in response to a violation of their sensitive character.

XVIII. TREE PEOPLE CAN BE VERY SENSITIVE TO COLD.

Just as they are sensitive to "bad" smells, trees are known to be sensitive to cold and dark weather. I immediately recognize my tree students by how tightly they rap their jackets around their bodies while hiding their noses inside their wooly scarves when the temperature drops down to fifty degrees. Metal and water people actually feel better in cold season weather, but trees loose a big chunk of their happy disposition the moment the sun is out and the cold descends. Trees usually have a few comfortable winter clothes which help them cope with cold temperatures, however because they are such fairy-like creatures who easily forget about important things, they often leave their warm clothes at home or in a car when they need them most. Trees often get colds and influenzas during late fall and winter and it takes them a longer time to recover, because the outside world is so "unfriendly."

XIX. TREE PEOPLE OFTEN HAVE DIFFICULTY ARRIVING ON TIME.

In the next chapter you will learn about the metal people, who often act as a direct opposite of the tree energy archetype. When it comes to being on time, trees and metals are opposites indeed. Metals are always on time (in fact a bit early), but trees will routinely arrive ten to fifteen minutes later *while thinking* they are on time. There is something unexplainable, in terms of rational thinking, in this infamous tendency of the trees to be unpredictable in terms of when they will arrive, depart, return your call, make an important decision, buy a ticket, and so forth. The best explanation I have come up with is that they are exactly like their counterparts in nature. We cannot make trees bloom according to our calendar. Even if they are very close to what we call spring blooming, the actual time when an individual cherry-tree or magnolia-tree is ready to go into blossom is only known to that tree alone.

And so it is with the tree people. We may think they are perfectly ready to go out with us. They are looking good and everything seems to be in place; a dress, a purse, a pair of shoes. But then the tree person says her shoes are not right. They hurt her feet and she must go change. When she changes shoes she realizes she cannot wear the same outfit and must change that. When the outfit is changed it requires new accessories with a different purse. By the time your beloved tree-person is ready to bloom for the public concert you are more than half an hour late.

XX. TREE PEOPLE ALWAYS WANT TO HELP OTHERS.

I open my 5-Element and Asian Religion classes by asking students what they want to do with their lives and what they plan on learning from the classes they are taking. Almost all metal people tell me they wish to accomplish certain personal goals. Compare this to how almost all trees say they want to help others! This is astounding!

Being a metal myself, every time I hear student after student saying they wish to save the animals, provide medical help to the poor, feed hungry people in Africa, or something like this, I feel the pangs in my consciousness. I am not suggesting that there are no metal people who help communities or that there are no tree people who are good at accomplishing goals. What I am saying is that unless trees think that they are helping others they find it difficult to become motivated. Just reaching certain goals is not good

Most nurses and caretakers have abundant tree energy

enough for them, but it is for most of us metals. This applies to how tree people study in college and how they live their lives. A tree student Galina says, "I do not like studying things which are too theoretical. I like to learn about things that can help other people. Unfortunately, just about every class from the Psychology department I have taken was very boring to me because they were all theory and no practice. I really liked this class in 5-elements, because I could tell immediately that this knowledge was going to be very useful for all my friends and relatives, as well as many, many other people. *When I don't think that what I am learning is going to help people I do not do well in such classes.* I cannot make myself study just for the sake of a good grade. Helping others makes me happy and it gives me a reason to work really hard."

Chapter Four

Metal People

People whose actions are ruled by the abundance of the metal energy receive the highest rate of approval from our society. Their only weaknesses are usually seen in traits they exhibit in personal relationships, not at work. It is most often in our love and friendships that we come across feelings hurt by the sharp edges and bossy attitudes of our metal partners. Also note that because in our society all males are trained in the ways of the Metal-energy, more men than women will have plenty of "metallic" features in their character.

If you the reader are born as a male, read carefully the following pages. Try to distinguish (if you can) between the forms of behavior which you have learned as a member of the American male culture and those behaviors which are your natural inclinations. To do so, it helps to remember how you used to act as a young boy, or how you may still act when you are alone when nobody sees you.

In addition to this, one must be aware that *all people, no matter what their innate element might be, acquire a substantial influx of the metal Qi when they reach their late thirties and forties.* (The process of how 5-elements affect our aging is explained further in chapter six.) So, whether you are an innate Metal, have developed it as a result of your male upbringing, or you simply have crossed over your thirty-fifth birthday mark, the following traits of the metal energy can be easily observed in your behavior as well as those whose lives are influenced by the Metal-Qi:

I. METAL PEOPLE ARE OBSESSED WITH ORDER.

I find this to be absolutely true for myself and other people who acknowledge their lives are influenced by an abundance of metal in their character. As you remember from the introduction, my second natural element is metal second only to fire, so I know everything about being that way. One way metals constantly irritate their friends or family members who are not metal elements is by their lack of personal flexibility, or refusal to accept other people's points of view and ways of doing things.

I confess that I am obsessed with getting my personal life and life around me arranged according to my order. Things must be done my way, or I cannot enjoy them. I actually refuse to participate in activities which do not correspond to my idea of how things should to be done.

Here is a confession from my metal friend Elena: "Things must be done according to my own plan, otherwise, I cannot enjoy my life. If I have planned to grade my students' papers until 12 o'clock on Sunday morning, I will stick to my plan no matter what. Even if my husband will come in and make the sweetest face and say, "I am so hungry, darling! Can't you take a short break, eat with me and then go back to grading?" I will answer: 'No way! If I stop now I will become distracted and not come back to grading after lunch, or if I return to it, my productivity will not be the same. And please, do not disturb me again or it will take me longer to finish."

Metals have a plan for everything and this plan must be followed. In this, they are not unlike the water-people who are attached to their routines. However, a water-person often forgets about what he wanted to do because he is easily distracted, but the metal person is practically never distracted from his or her goal.

II. Metals have a deeply rooted need to have places of work and residence to be clean and perfectly organized.

Most metals prefer (some must have) their places of work and residence completely clean and neat otherwise, they find it difficult to function. One of my metallic students shared in class that she cannot start doing her homework if her house is not clean. To the non-metallic students this sounded very strange. How is the cleanliness of the house related to writing a paper? But for metals it is! Believe me, in our world of the metallic mind, it all makes sense. Here is how it works for me; if the house is not clean and my room is not organized, I cannot concentrate on my project. I will be looking at the dust-balls under the bed or a big ugly spot on the carpet every five minutes, thinking it must be fixed, and will not be able to keep my mind on what I am writing.

III. Metals enjoy classifying things according to specific categories.

This is absolutely true. My metal friend Irene has the most perfectly organized closet in the whole world. In one closet section she keeps only short dresses while the opposite corner contains only long dresses and long skirts, the two sections never mix. Not once have I seen Irene not knowing where to go in her closet to find the right dress for an adventure she had planned.

My dear friend Jeff Primack tells people that in an "extreme metal" person's kitchen, spice racks are organized in alphabetical order. When he says this everybody laughs because it is funny, yet it is absolutely true! As a metal person I am ashamed to admit that inside my kitchen drawer, spoons/forks are organized based on their length. Go figure!

68

For strong metal types a clean desk is mandatory

IV. METALS ARE VERY BOSSY AND LOVE BEING IN CHARGE OF THINGS AND PEOPLE.

Mea culpa! As a metal, I love to act as if I am in charge of everything. Regardless of whether other people can or cannot make their own decisions, I love making decisions for them, and I often think my decisions to be so much better than theirs.

Metals love being in charge of other people's dating, marriages, divorces, job searches, house haunting, pet selection, religious practices, and so on. Metals will actively engage in other people's lives regardless of whether they have been asked for help or not. On the positive side, because metals are so good at searching, organizing and helping, people often ask them for help or advice. When metals are being asked for help or advice, they feel really good about it and their sense of self-worthiness grows. Be aware there is an important difference between how the tree person helps others and how the metal does. When a metal is asked for help, they immediately begin exercising personal authority over the person who requested their help. It is as if the mind of a metallic person says, "If you want me to help you, you must surrender to my will, accept my control over the whole situation, and allow me to be in charge of everything because believe me, this is the only way things are going to work between you and me."

By comparison, trees begin their rescue operations without any specific plan, and instead of exuding authority they exude self-sacrifice. Both of these methods work for different people and different situations. Just be aware that helping others can be a totally different endeavor depending on the innate elements of people involved.

V. Metals have a fondness for Sour they love Eating raw limes, cranberries, pickles, sour cream, or sour candies.

While dining together with a metal person, you may notice they often reach for foods with a sour, vinegary taste. Someone who can eat pickles straight out of a jar or finishes a container of marinated olives or pepperoncinies in less than a week is definitely blessed with the metallic Qi. This preference for the pickled, sour taste rather than sweetness sets metals apart from the tree energy and often saves them from being overweight (their remarkable ability to be on schedule and exercise also helps). However, this uncanny love for the sour stuff spreads beyond food and drinks as metals tend to see many things in a sourly way making their usual comments and jokes not terribly sweet either.

VI. Metal people cannot stand it when other people become emotional.

One of my students expressed this perfectly: "I am so happy to learn that all people with metal energy resent it when others cry or break down emotionally. I thought for a long time I was a bad person because every time my girl-friend cried I could not stand it. What I mean is that my first impulse was to run out of the house, let her cry as much as she wanted and come back when she was normal. But when I did this the situation got worse. She told me that I was a

The metal person has difficulty listening to someone cry

monster because 'when people are crying, others should try to understand their situation.' But I disagreed. I couldn't just sit, listening to her complaints. If I knew who hurt her I just need to talk to that person and stop them from doing it again. And if I hurt her I just want to apologize and be done with it. But this is not what she wants. She can stay in that "wet moodiness," as I call it, for hours, which makes me hate her. But now that I know that I am a metal and she is a tree, I must work on developing my own tree energy. Then I will be able to listen to her and know how to act when she cries."

VII. Metal energy makes people appreciate and strongly enjoy things with symmetric patterns.

When we walk into a metal person's apartment or house, we will notice that not only is everything neat and clean but there is also a persistent symmetrical arrangement observed throughout the space. For instance, towels of matching colors will hang parallel to each other on the rack. A lamp in one corner of the room will be somehow balanced by another lamp in the opposite corner. Tables and chairs will be in perfect symmetry with each other. And there will be plenty of matching colors everywhere from walls to towels, from lamps to place-mats.

Metal people go to the store with a piece of fabric they want to match and they return objects simply because they did not match the color. If you share your life with such a metal person, it probably drives you nuts, especially if a metal person is a woman dressing for a party. But male metals can be just as annoying when they buy appliances.

The non-metal people must understand that living in a state of symmetry and matching colors gives metal people a sense of security. Metal energy feels stronger in this geometrically symmetric and color-matched universe, this is very different from how trees and fires feel about it. Fires and trees actually feel suffocated and irritated by a visible display of order and the authoritarianism present in the symmetrical patterns. Just as sacred geometry enhances the flow of the divine power from God to people, the so called "mundane geometry" is also about enhancing power, but usually it is the power of those who are in charge of a social situation. Think about military buildings and troop formations, about classrooms and parking lots, prisons and court rooms. None of these spaces are organized in a spontaneous, chaotic or free flowing manner. The reason why? It is much easier to maintain control over people when they are locked inside simple geometric shapes such as a squares and rectangles.

On a lighter note, metals feel intuitively they must wear clothes and accessories with matching colors and symmetric patterns, all the way from their hair to their socks. Metals will not wear a rose skirt with a green jacket. This is for a tree person and is nearly a blasphemy for a metal. White tops with dark bottoms, or any variation of the simplest of all symmetrical designs is a favorite with all metals. If a metal person has water as their second element, which is often the case, they will favor black, grey and blue colors. But if the metal person's second element is Fire, which is also a rather widespread phenomenon, the white top may be exchanged for red, purple or black.

VIII. METALS ARE OFTEN COMPETITIVE THEY LIKE TO PARTICIPATE IN ACTIVITIES WHEN THEY KNOW THEY CAN WIN.

Our society approves of the metal energy's patterns of behavior more than that of the other four elements. Competition, which naturally develops in a metal person's character, has now become a foundation of our culture. In our schools we teach children how to compete, have high scores and win awards upon entering the first grade. Those who have plenty of innate metal Qi are doing really well in such competitive education, but children with other elements including waters, trees and fires are not as well prepared for this kind of training.

The first thing you will notice about a metal person who enjoys competing is that they will never enter a competition without a plan to win. If they are sure they are going to loose they will reset the terms of engagement, making it appear they are the winners. Metals leave the task of sticking to a cause without hope of winning for those people who are born with the tree energy. Trees will usually remain in a hopeless relationship or other unpleasant situation out of the sheer kindness in their hearts, but metals will not do that. This would seem to them to be a loss of their precious time. Instead they look for a device or plan to allow them to overcome the difficulty so they can feel triumphant. Needless to say, all sport and business celebrities in our society have plenty of metal Qi in their character.

IX. Metals are big on justice and think of themselves as always being right.

If you have a friend who always argues with you no matter what you share or propose, you need to know this person is ruled by the innate power of metal Qi. She or he will not stop arguing with others until their character changes later in life under the influence of the element water (read chapter six on the life span of when elements are prominent). When metals argue, it is not about whether what you say makes sense or not, it goes much deeper and therefore much more difficult for you to change. If you understand the simple fact that metal kitchen knives become sharper when you clash them against each other, you can also understand why the metal people enjoy arguing so much. For them it is almost the same as eating chocolates and smiling at each other (as it is for the tree people).

Usually people endowed with metal element do not reflect on their actual enjoyment during the process of arguing. They argue because they believe they are right, while others are wrong and need to be corrected. *Metal people don't realize those who they argue against are psychologically suffering in these "corrective" discussions and looking for ways to avoid them.*

Metals lack introspective qualities, and honestly believe they are always right. They feel justified in taking strong actions based on their beliefs, yet if one observes carefully, they will notice that a metal person's positions shift, changing frequently. What they believed was right yesterday may not be the same thing they say is right today, but their memory does not recognize it! Metals must believe they are always right in order to carry on with their duties.

X. Metals Respect Laws, Rules & Regulations When, Occasionally, They Break Them... They Justify It As Being Necessary For A Greater Cause.

Metals always talk about following rules. They have an easy time following instructions of any kind and obeying the law, which cannot be said about people who are endowed with abundance of the fire or tree energy. Sometimes metals can be too preoccupied with rules and regulations, missing more important aspects of a relationship or situation. Metals however are capable of going against the rules when convinced it is not right. They will launch a campaign in order to do away with a regulation that doesn't seem right to them. You are correct if you think metal-people make perfect lawyers and executives. During my lifetime which is more than half a century long, and spans across five continents, I have not met a single person successful in jurisprudence who did not possess an overly metallic personality, at least in the place of work.

XI. Metals Enjoy Having And Displaying Personal Strength, Especially Through Muscles And Physical Fitness.

Metals must experience strength and tightness of their muscles in order to feel good. Unlike waters and trees, who do not share this particular fondness for the well developed muscles, metals have an obsession with it. As I mentioned earlier, our society prefers metal behavior to other energy archetypes. This is why this particular state of the human body – all muscles, no soft rolls – became a beauty ideal. This ideal of beauty did not exist in medieval times when humans were not allowed to practice their metal

Extreme metal types may be obsessed with physical fitness

energy except when they became warriors or soldiers. During that time most of the population, especially women, were not allowed to feel proud of their physical strength, and both genders were not supposed to view well developed muscles as objects of an aesthetical appreciation. This is because a strong and perfectly shaped body often becomes a source of pride and selfishness. Metals often have great bodies to a disciplined fitness routine, and for the most part are somewhat proud, self-absorbed people. Extreme metal types may spend hours and hours everyday just to build and display their muscles. Even common knowledge that this kind of body-building is not good for one's health does not seem to have an affect on them.

Metal people have an uncanny ability to exude self-confidence through their physical appearance and outwardly hide any signs of doubt they may have in a situation. No matter what happens around them they will continue acting as if they are in charge. Even when things go badly they will not admit it verbally nor will they show it physically. This is a stark contrast to the behavior of tree people who appear visibly anxious and uncertain even when things are going well for them. This is true even if everyone involved is loving and respecting towards them.

XII. METALS ARE VERY GOOD WITH MONEY.

People born with metal energy are capable of saving money regardless of how much or little of it they earn. For example, children born with the metal-Qi will ask their parents for more chores to earn a bigger allowance or start doing work for their neighbors, earning their first income while they are still in school. These children intuitively know how to put money away and resist the temptation to spend it. When I look at the lives of adults endowed with metal Qi, including myself, I observe that we share this uncanny ability to generate "golden coins" out of everything we do and hold to our fortunes. While other elements are not naturally possessed with our same ease of making money. When we see other elements prospering financially there is usually a person with metal who is involved as an advisor or banker of some kind.

XIII. METALS ARE DRAWN TO SCIENCE. THEY APPRECIATE A SCIENTIFIC WORLDVIEW OVER RELIGIOUS/NON-PHYSICAL VIEWPOINTS

Metals are in love with science. In fact, we have to thank (or curse, depending on what element you are ☺) people endowed with the metallic character for successfully bringing down the age of mythology and begetting the new era where everything must be measured and rationally explained in order to be considered a part of reality.

Metals love to measure & compare what they've measured. These two simple actions, "measuring and comparing", have become the foundation of scientific thinking. If something cannot be seen, or measured at any given moment by an 'instrument' ~ it is not real. This is the perspective of many metal scientists like James Randi, who offers a million dollar reward to anyone who can prove the paranormal or existence of Qi. He has upset many masters, because he is never convinced and has never paid anyone. Of course, his worldview is extra rigid into the physical matter only. Many metal scientists are not this way and instead believe in a higher power or spirit that animates our physical forms. Yet, because of metals' strong interest in "real world' results, they can sometimes miss the more subtle (sub-physical) aspects of creation, energy, emotions, spirit etc.

People of strong metal character have shaped our perception of the world through science. The poetic and artistic ways of connecting to the world that are associated with tree, fire and water personalities are being pushed away, becoming second in importance. But are they really that unimportant? Our metal readers may wish to think on this.

Physical things like a person's hormone levels and the size of their poop can tell us a lot about a person's health. Emotions cannot be measured in a laboratory, but if someone is sick it may be coming from an emotional cause. Strong metal types of people like to discredit this view on medicine claiming it is not scientific. This is because emotional causes of disease cannot be measured under a microscope as easily as hormones. Yet, the statistical facts of people who get cancer one year after a severe emotional trauma speaks volumes about the truth of science. If science or metal people only pay attention to what they can measure, perhaps they will miss a crucial part of the equation.

XIV. METAL PEOPLE HAVE NO DIFFICULTY LIVING THEIR LIVES ACCORDING TO A SCHEDULE.

Metal people are always punctual, arriving on time. In fact, they prefer to arrive a few minutes early, because they hate being late. They also follow through on their promises and agreements nearly one hundred per cent. This of course provides little tolerance on the part of the metals for those who are often late for appointments, forget about their promises or make promises they are unable to deliver. These are typical tree and fire people's behavior.

Metals love science because it's truth must be measurable

One particular trait that helps with metals' punctuality and their ability to remember promises is their naturally good memory. Metals treasure their ability to remember so highly, that if they think they may forget something they will find a way to remind themselves what they do not wish to forget. While there are many social and personal benefits from this natural gift, it may also work against the metal people when they have hard time forgetting things they truly wish to forget.

XV. METALS LOVE TO BE CHALLENGED.

Not only do metals respond well to naturally challenging situations (unlike the tree and water people who do not function well under pressure) they actually enjoy creating conflict bound situations for themselves in order to boost their energy and maximize their performance. Competition is a very metallic way of accomplishing things and it also creates the very challenge metals may need to dedicate their time entirely to one goal. Metal people might give themselves a challenge by declaring a deadline for their project. They may announce the completion of their project to their superiors, customers, friends, or publishers to add even more pressure so they are motivated to work even harder. *When the deadline is set then not finishing the product by the declared date would be a disaster.* So the metal person applies all her or his energy toward completing the project on time thereby succeeding where others might have failed. Jeff and I are both metals and we love to work under the extreme pressure of a deadline. At the same time, I know hundreds of people who absolutely cannot function well if there is a time-sensitive pressure to finish.

To reach an even higher level of personal growth and social engagement, some metals push themselves into thinking that they must become the best, or the very least reach the top level in their entire field of activities. As they attempt to reach the imaginary goal of number one, their productivity rises tremendously and they accomplish a lot. Metals do not realize that other elements do not see the world in the same way they do and for this reason refuse to compete with them. When other people do not wish to compete, metals can make the mistake of thinking of them as less skillful or less intelligent.

XVI. METALS LIKE TO MAKE LISTS OF THINGS TO DO.

I would say this is a typical metal person's way of ordering the world to their liking, and making their lives useful at the same time. As a metal person makes a long list of things she must do during a day, checking them off one by one, she experiences a sense of relief and a certain victory. She feels that life has meaning and she has power to control it. Because making lists and seeing them done is so psychologically soothing for the metals many of them love creating such "to-do" lists for every month of the year and every year of their life. Nothing can upset a metal person more than a complete impossibility on their "to do" list.

XVII. METALS CAN BE AGGRESSIVE.

Some metals are naturally militant and aggressive and how they feel about the world shows in their behavior. They may enjoy sparring or wrestling with someone. Related to this is metals (including females) mysterious fondness for weapons, especially metal weapons such as the superb Katana swords used by Japanese samurais, or a really powerful knife. They can be also drawn to rifles and pistols, and I can say for certain that lots of metal energy stands behind the National Rifle Association and its activities.

Metals of course are excellent at shooting all types of targets. Some prefer a legal shooting range while others enjoy knocking down empty glass-bottles in a desert or the mountains. Shooting actually makes metal people more restful and relaxed and they should do more of it (provided it's safe for others). If they do there is less need for their external aggression towards other people.

We must also comment that there is a huge difference between the metallic and fire aggression. Fire's aggression seems to come out of nowhere, like an explosion, in response to something others may have a hard time seeing as a viable reason for acting so crazy. Also, the fire person's rage although unpredictable and vicious, can quickly divert to something else or simply end. By comparison the metallic rage has more, so to speak, logic. One can predict when and why it is coming, usually when the metal person's power and authority have been challenged. For some metals who abuse their power, there is a *clear pattern* they follow every time. This may allow a potential victim of the metal's abuse to take measures to defend him or herself. However, people who find themselves within the abusive range of a fire person's new explosion of rage may not have such luck.

XVIII. METALS CANNOT STAND DEFEAT.

If metal people think they have lost, no matter how insignificant the loss may be, they become depressed and unable to function normally for a while or even a long time. Joshua, a metal student admits, "It does not matter whether I am really well prepared for an exam or I cheat, I must have an outstanding grade on all of my exams. If I score less than

B+ at school I hate myself and get depressed for several days. I do work hard, but sometimes I cannot know all the answers and this drives me nuts because I must win no matter what."

On the other side of metal's innate intolerance for personal defeats lies their desire to celebrate all their victories. They do so with a most serious dedication as they collect and display for others to see all marks of personal distinction, such as awards, trophies, medals, prizes, diplomas, certificates, and so on. Even brief compliments from their superiors make metal people feel proud and they are more than likely to share this news with their family and friends. The seriousness with which metals take compliments and awards can often make them the laughing stock of other elements. Especially in the eyes of the fire people, who do not care about social prestige for its own sake, but rather as a form of protection of their freedom to do what they want.

Related to this, is a metal person's commitment to winning at any cost. It can be a very positive trait as scientists, artists and sport champions refuse to give up despite strong odds against them, accomplishing the unthinkable. But it can be also very negative as this gut-felt need for victory may lead to deceit, treachery, and other anti-social behavior.

XIX. METALS ALWAYS PROTECT THEIR INTERESTS AS WELL AS THE INTERESTS OF THOSE WHOM THEY CONSIDER TO BE THEIR "TRIBE."

Metals are not shy or easily intimidated people (unless their second element is water or they have a lot of it in their character). They stand in stark contrast with the tree and water people, who are so shy or considerate of other people's feelings that they may not ask a clerk at a store where the bathroom is located even when the need to use it is pressing upon them. But the metal person's combativeness grows to a whole new level when they feel they are fighting for a just cause which protects their self-interest and the interests of those whom they have taken under their protection such as spouses, parents, children, co-workers, members of their church, their ethnic group, and so on.

As metals try to defend people of their own "tribe" they often go into offensive mode, driven by strong emotions of resistance, anger and sometimes hate toward people from "another tribe" against whom they are protecting their own people. Metals do not hesitate to display strong emotions publicly perhaps accusing opposing tribes of crimes which they are sure they have committed. But more than likely their accusations are based on the fact that they are different from their own tribe.

This polarized thinking, often present in metal's character becomes amplified due to their sense of urgency in their fight for justice. As a result, metals always overdo their punishment expeditions against the perceived perpetrators. Metals usually lack the empathy that would allow them the ability to the feel pain and frustration of other people. This is why they tend to turn the punishment of the guilty into a "justice campaign" where victory must be won over an enemy. But exactly who the enemy is and what that victory might be remains unclear. Therefore, conflicts instigated by metals always grow from small & insignificant to ones of larger, grander fashion until exhaustion of resources is reached (the so called rusting of metal) halting the conflict and temporarily restoring balance.

XX. METAL PEOPLE CAN BE UNMOVED BY OTHER PEOPLE'S PAIN AND SUFFERING.

This may sound like a negative character flaw, but this is not necessarily true. Let me explain using an example from my training with my Buddhist teacher; When he was teaching me how to build relationships with other people, (especially the opposite gender) to whom I was attracted, he explained that pain and suffering would come if I created my own relationship ideal. This ideal he said, would be projected onto the other person's behavior. He was teaching me how to love and respect without developing intellectual and emotional attachment. It took me a long time to learn this lesson. Every time I would come to him crying, screaming and cursing my boy-friend's horrible behavior he would just smile and say, "You have chosen suffering yet again. You have chosen pain because you still think you can change your beloved, but he will not change. He will not change unless he chooses to change. No amount of your suffering will make it possible. You are just wasting your time." He would then turn his back to me and walk away no matter how great my pain was. He would not give me a hug or say a single nice word; only a reminder of what I already knew.

When parents discipline their children they too must exercise strong metal qualities in their character in order to enforce house rules on a child who may feel terribly hurt or wronged by the people he loves. For if the parents give up, it is possible that the child can ruin the entire family.

On the negative side, we see metal's innate belief that leads them to believe they are always right and the other person is wrong, but this just isn't so! So, if a metal person is positive they are in the right, (but in fact they aren't) and they continue disciplining and punishing someone who they think needs it, the abuse can be devastating. We must also remind our readers what we have already said about metals in general; they don't act well in the presence of those in emotional upheaval, particularly when someone is crying. Metals ability for empathy is lower than the other elements. They *are simply unable* to feel the same degree of emotional drama and pain as people with other elements usually do. When we remember this, our interpersonal communications may become much more beautiful and ultimately satisfying.

Chapter Five

Earth People

There are more people born with the Earth element than any other. This is because Earth elements are the balance-keepers in our society. They help us other elements to better understand ourselves and one another. Without them, the internal conflicts between water and fire, as well as tree and metal would become too strong, tearing the fabric of our lives apart. Although the Earth element has its own distinct characteristics, they may be too subtle for most of us to detect. *The Earth's characteristics are not juxtaposed to any specific element the same way water opposes fire and metal opposes tree.* However, after you read this chapter you will be able to recognize Earth people in your life, including yourself.

I. WHEN EARTH ELEMENT LEARNS ABOUT FIRE, WATER, TREE AND METAL PEOPLE, THEY CANNOT DECIDE WHO THEY ARE.

Discovering this is one sure way to recognize someone with innate Qi of Earth. Thomas, an Earth-student explained: "I definitely share some of the fire, water, tree and metal patterns in my life, but I definitely do not share all of them! When one of my friends who is fire says, "Let's go have some beer and then jump from the roof into my swimming pool!" I say, "I will have beer, but I am not jumping and you shouldn't jump either man, because it is stupid." He jumps anyway but I can never be as fiery as he is. My other friend, who is water, wants to play video games for days in a row! Like, literally he won't get out of the house for two days if he likes the game. I can play for six hours max and then I am done. I must get out and do something. At same time I think I am like metal and tree. For example, I enjoy sweet things and I can be very organized if I must, but I would not go into any of these people's extremes. I guess this does make me an Earth person, and just as you said, this makes Earth people the balance keepers."

II. EARTH PEOPLE HAVE HARD TIME DECIDING WHAT TO DO WITH THEIR LIVES.

The Earth people are balancers that keep everything and everyone in some sort of peaceful harmony with each other, however they have a hard time finding their own goals. Unlike fire, they do not become passionate about one particular thing. Unlike trees, they are not sure their goal is to help serve other people. Unlike metals, they find it boring to set up goals and see them accomplished. And unlike water, they are not withdrawn and self-absorbed enough to stop caring about the outer world altogether.

"The Earth students in my classes usually sigh with relief upon the realization there are plenty of Earth-people like them in this world. The honorable excuse of "being balanced" explains why they have such difficulty finding what makes them tick. When there is no extreme in ANY direction it is harder to see any clear identifying tendencies toward being heavier in one element."

Earth-people will participate in whatever is available at the moment. They bide their time waiting to see what God sends their way. This can be a challenge though, because on

Earth people often have trouble deciding on a career

one hand Earth people feel their vitality and readiness for action, but on the other hand, nothing CALLS TO THEM strongly enough to propel them into serious action.

"Earths must learn how to follow subtle clues and be happy with gentle forms of inspiration," decided Mary, an Earth student, and I think she is right. Earth element's "inertia" is infamous, but different from the near complete passivity then resignation to an inner world the water-people experience. Waters prefer to be withdrawn and are not in pain, or great doubt about their passive ways.

Earths can fully relate to the powers of all other elements. They crave the social successes common to metals and fires, and often beat themselves up for being too lazy or not accomplishing enough with their lives.

III. EARTHS DO NOT LIKE ANYTHING THAT GOES INTO EXCESS OR EXTREME.

If you think about it, this is a very useful trait the Earth people naturally possess. As Thomas explained previously, Earths try to stop their crazy friends from jumping off the roof, or at least they will have enough character to avoid the danger themselves, which the tree people who are friends with the fires may not have. Earths also prevent their tree friends from getting too emotional or too charitable. And they stop their water friends from sitting alone in their rooms all day long. However, this seemingly positive trait can have a negative impact on the lives of the Earth-people. Sometimes we must go to extremes to accomplish things. Like letting our sacred fire burn, or allowing our dutiful metal to work non-stop to finish a book or stay by the side of a person we really love and wish to spend the rest of our lives with, but the Earth person cannot do this. This fact often leaves them with a kind of sadness in their hearts, as if they always stop short of accomplishing something important, short of reaching a goal. I often hear from my Earth-friends, "I was just so close to getting it done and then I felt like I didn't care anymore." Or, "I simply wanted to go back to how things were before we started our relationship. I was so tired of its challenges, it became unimportant."

Earths must remember that they are a gift to the community. Even if they do not accomplish any lofty goals, their support to humanity is irreplaceable. If they choose to accept this fact, they will be less self-critical and much happier people as a result.

Earth people make the best support persons or team-players. By supporting others they shine, becoming quite glorious.

IV. EARTH PEOPLE PREFER BLAND, NEUTRAL TASTES IN EVERYTHING, INCLUDING FOOD AND FASHION.

If you are a fire person, this particular trait of the Earths may drive you nuts. Because Earths love a bland taste, what they choose to wear often appears tasteless to fires and even some trees. To the metals, the Earths' way of dressing appears too casual and not neat enough. Earths do not enjoy wearing clothes that stand out in a crowd. This means the Earths often do not appear chic or strikingly sexy.

Fire person Mark, speaks about his Earth girl-friend Mara; "She has a perfect figure and is good-looking, but she just does not know how to dress. No matter what she wears it all looks like a bunch of potato sacks. Pants and tops are baggy in some weird brown colors. It was not until I learned in your class that she is Earth element I realized that this was not because she does not know how to dress, but because she really feels comfortable in these brownish shapeless things she calls "comfortable clothes." Here is my question for you professor, can the Earth girl be trained to wear fashionable clothes?"

In the margins of Mark's paper, I wrote: "Earth is resistant and has the power to wear the fire people out. Just learn how to compromise. Help your girlfriend find clothes that are not too crazy or too tight on her body and she will wear them."

V. EARTH PEOPLE ARE SOMETIMES REALLY GOOD AT PROCRASTINATING.

Sometimes I ask myself; who is a better procrastinator, an Earth or a water person? My answer is the Earth and here is why; Water people when asked to do something, won't do it, end of story. But Earth-people have enough social consciousness to remember what their friends and relatives asked them to do and they really want to help out. Yet, they will continue delaying the fulfillment of their promises for days and even months. Do you see what I mean? With the Earth, the process of not delivering promises is more complicated for it is prolonged and charged with psychological drama. The water person's ultimately passive behavior is well known, therefore expectations are low. But when we are dealing with the Earth person it is unpredictable, because sometimes they find enough strength to carry on according to plan and other times they sabotage it for a very long time while continuously giving us hopes. Because it drags on and on, it eventually leaves whoever must deal with the Earth element (especially if this person is metal!) depleted and tired, creating a clear and long living memory of procrastination.

We need to remember however, that *all of us* become procrastinators from time to time, like the Earth element can sometimes demonstrate. Procrastination is our natural defense against the pressures and demands of modern society. Still, someone who has Earth as their natural element engages in this form of behavior rather regularly.

VI. EARTH PEOPLE FIND IT EASY TO AGREE WITH EVERYONE ELSE.

Having come this far in the book, you can probably predict the reactions of fire, metal, water and tree people may have to words or *situations they do not agree with*.

Fire will probably say,
"This is crap," or
"I don't care who said this but I don't buy it…"

Metal will go into a reasonable critical analysis of the position offered, winning the debate.

Tree will either feel emotionally hurt or try to be nice to the person despite the fact they don't like what is been proposed.

Water person may say nothing or say very little and still find no pressure to contribute in any significant way.

The Earth person's response is different from all of the above. This is because -- we must remember this -- Earth can act as one of the other four elements or it can act as its own element with its own distinct characteristics. When presented with a new and possibly unpleasant life scenario, the Earth person is capable of reaching beyond their natural preferences, finding grains of truth in almost any words, actions or ideological platforms. Earth will be able to see that what was proposed has *some* value and *some* potential so they give their silent or verbal support, greatly surprising others sitting at the negotiation table. However, even though Earth people can relate to lots of different ideas and propositions, they do not feel obligated to follow them in their lives or support them through their actions.

VII. EARTHS LIKE SOIL, MUD, CLAY, AND HAVE A STRONG LIKING FOR DIGGING HOLES IN THE GROUND. PLANTING TREES, MAKING POTTERY, AND SCULPTING MAY BE HEALING FOR THEM.

Although the Earth people are usually pretty laid back, some may even say lazy, they can create opportunities to connect to their innate element Earth, through all sorts of activities. They may take a college art class which requires working with clay, or unintentionally join a community garden, or simply help neighbors with their plants. One way or another, Earths find ways to get dirty and all covered in their innate element, and this is good for them.

An Earth person Peter remarks on his fondness for mud, "Every time I am surrounded by mud, just mud, without glamorous gardening or other stuff people do in the ground, I feel very happy."

VIII. EARTHS LIKE BEING IN THE MIDDLE OF THINGS, BUT NEVER TOO INVOLVED OR COMMITTED.

If you pay attention to the Earth's behavior you may become amused, just like I am, when you realize that the

Earths like making pottery, digging holes and planting trees

Earth element enjoys being in the middle of the action, but not truly involved in it. What I mean by that is that the Earth people will stick around for parties, celebrations, concerts, events of all sorts, and yet they somehow avoid initiating such events by themselves. In this respect they are almost similar to water-people. The difference would be that waters do not appreciate when people talk in loud voices, in fact they actually do not like talking at all. Because many social events requite talking and interacting, waters avoid going at all. They participate only when they can get away with zero talking and participation. To watch and observe, this is the water's motto. But Earths are different. They are not withdrawn from social aggression to the same degree as the water element is. Earths actually enjoy good conversation, even with strangers, provided they are not the ones who initiated and it requires no further commitment on their part.

Due to this unique feature of their innate character, Earth people often find themselves in a middle of a college, family or workplace romantic drama, where a small circle of people get upset about each other and begin gossiping and punishing each other for "inappropriate behavior." Almost inevitably there is an Earth person in the circle who listens to everybody complain, knows everyone's side of the story, but stays away from forming moral judgment, taking sides or becoming fully involved.

IX. EARTH PEOPLE ARE GOOD AT FINDING A SPECIAL, COMFORTABLE PLACE ON A BED, COUCH OR CHAIR.

Now this is uncanny. Earths just know where this special spot on a bed, chair or couch is located, so that when you lie there, half-reclined, you feel like Buddha in the state

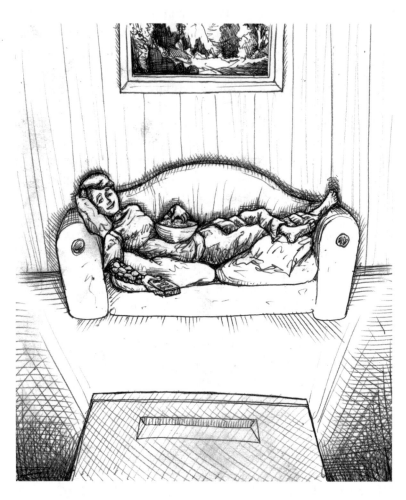

Earth people are experts at relaxing

of nirvana. Your body silently murmuring, "M-mm...how come this feels so good?" Earths usually have a special place in the room, where they remain in their relaxed, Buddha-like posture for long hours each day (or as often as they can) reading a book, watching TV or playing with the computer. Once again their behavior is similar to that of the water people. The difference may appear subtle or significant depending on what element you are. Earth can sit in front of the TV for three hours, but then become bored requiring immediate action. Water may sit in front of a computer playing their favorite video game for seven or eight hours straight even holding back the desire to use the bathroom.

X. EARTHS HAVE SPECIAL APPRECIATION FOR FOODS WITH A BLAND TASTE AND ARE ESPECIALLY FOND OF ROOT VEGETABLES.

We all love the taste of potato dishes such as French fries, potato chips and mashed potatoes. This is because we grew up in the United States or became accustomed to this country's ubiquitous potato-cooking. American culture has a very strong earth element to it, and the potato is indigenous to American soil. However, in the innate Earth element, love of the potato taste becomes magnified. An Earth person can literally eat potatoes, in one form or another, every day of the year. But they don't eat other types of foods every day, such as fish, grapes, sauerkraut, tomatoes, or spicy chilly soup.

Similarly, Earth people have a fondness for other foods with a neutral taste such as rice and bread. Almost all Earth people find at some point in their life a particular type of bread, which they are able to enjoy so much that they can eat it alone. Just as in all other forms of their behavior, Earths do not appreciate tastes that are too extreme. They do not eat anything that is too hot, sour or bitter.

XI. EARTHS DON'T FEEL THE NEED TO BE CLEAN ALL THE TIME.

This may be a sensitive stuff, but I will say it anyway. People who are born with natural element of earth do not like keeping their bodies exceptionally clean. I mean their bodies naturally resist the idea of taking two showers a day, washing their hair every day, changing into new clothes every day and so on. People who enjoy and actually need this type of exceptionally clean life-style are known at this point -they are the metal element.

Earths are different from metal. They like wearing the same clothes the next day. They do not mind some smells, but will use the deodorant just for the sake of others if they care enough about them.

XII. EARTHS PEOPLE GET ROMANTICALLY INVOLVED WITH WHOEVER IS AVAILABLE AT THE MOMENT.

You probably remember that fires experience the need to chase after their relationships and that difficulties attract them. Not so with the Earth people. They definitely *do not* enjoy chasing after their potential mate and for this reason you can recognize someone as a typical Earth person by looking at their dating patterns. If every time they go to a different university (or get a new job) and become romantically involved with the man or woman living on the same floor or no more than 15 minutes away, you are dealing with an Earth person!

XIII. EARTHS OFTEN DISLIKE COMPETITIVE SPORTS OR ANY COMPETITIVE ACTIVITIES FOR THAT MATTER.

Once again, Earth is almost the opposite of metal. Metals need competitions to keep them involved, but for the Earths this is a big turn off. The moment things become too competitive they will drop off the project. Earths can be recognized as people who do not care enough about promotions, salary raises or fighting for educational and professional marks of distinction. Unfortunately, for this very reason they are not valued or promoted by people in leading positions who see the Earth personality as lacking ambition. In our society, personal ambition is the driving force behind success, so Earth people usually remain in the secondary posts. Because the Earth people do not enjoy fighting or conquering they too will settle for less, accepting a position lower than what they deserve.

XIV. EARTH PEOPLE USUALLY HAVE SOME ARTISTIC TALENT, BUT DO NOT SERIOUSLY COMMIT TO PURSUING IT.

Earth people are gifted from birth. Things come easy to them. This is why; in Asian communities parents calculate dates for their intimacy in order to give birth to children with the Earth Qi (i.e. years ending in 8 and 9). But because the Earth children are good in just about everything they do, they do not really know what it means to fight for something and do not have or develop the skills they lack. As a result, in the realm of arts, including visual arts and music, where Earths have a substantial natural gift, metals usually accomplish more than the Earths do.

Here is a description from Robert, "It helped me a great deal to realize that, as the Earth person, I can relate to everything and can do just about anything. Because everything I try I am good at, I never felt like I wanted to work harder. I see how other students, who have less natural talent than I, excel in their art projects, because they work on them really hard. Even if they lack originality and real creativity, which my friends say I have plenty of, their projects end up being somehow better than mine."

XV. EARTH PEOPLE ARE BRIGHT AND YET NOT VERY GOOD AT MAKING JUDGMENTS OR SERIOUS DECISIONS.

This is one of those cases where the good becomes the bad and vice versa. Because Earths are the balancers and can reach out and understand the other four elements' positions, they have difficulty formulating the necessary judgments for themselves. I am not talking about discriminatory judgments, but rather discernment. It is necessary for all of us at some point to decide whether we choose to go on with someone's plan when we know that this person's schemes may hurt other people. Or do we choose to pursue career of our own despite a dear friend of ours who is trying to create an opposition to this decision.

Earths are not very good when it comes to these scenarios. As a result they often become stuck in some unpleasant affair which does not allow them to show their absolute best. They may unconsciously support people who are not of a good moral character or disallow moral people from implementing the necessary changes for improvement of a work or family situation.

XVI. Earth people have a particular sense of humor.

Earths have an "Earthy" sense of humor, which other elements may find to be not so kosher. Most of the American comedy shows are based on the type of humor that the Earth element favors. This is why fires and waters find less to laugh at when they watch comedies with their Earth friends. Earths however, will laugh at almost anything from the American movie industry or TV comedy shows.

When making personal jokes and telling anecdotes, Earth people enjoy saying things that can make the tree person cringe and blush. They tell jokes involving physiology, human or animal, or something that has just the right amount element of "dirt" in it. This can be compared to "black humor" jokes, which the water people favor, but are a bit too much for the Earth. Fires who of course also love to laugh, must find their own comedies. The ones favored by the Earth aren't biting enough.

XVII. Earths often feel uncomfortable in highly elevated places and may be afraid of heights.

Well, waters are afraid of heights as well, but waters usually keep a low profile in everything they do, so this particular fear of theirs does not become a point of public observation. Earths try to experience everything in life, at least once, and they usually find their fear of heights in a hard and painful way – in front of everyone. Because they are so talented and can do many things so easily, they may think that flying or sky-diving are not going to be a big deal for them, but because it involves dealing with heights where the Earth person's body must be significantly elevated above the Earth level they will feel great psychological and physiological discomfort. Some Earth people can overcome this, especially if she or he has enough fire in their character. At the same time, all Earths love hiking and climbing mountains when it is done on their own terms and with accommodating speed.

XVIII. GETTING MATERIAL SUPPORT IS RELATIVELY EASY FOR EARTH PEOPLE, BUT BECOMING FINANCIALLY POWERFUL IS NOT.

Earths always have a relatively easy time getting their basic needs covered. There is something almost magical in how God and the universe reach out to them when help is needed, as if the Earths are being thanked for all the balancing and harmonizing they bring to others. Yet, when Earths wish to acquire more money-power they may run into problems. Although it seems easy, (as metal is dug out of the Earth) the natural inclinations of the Earth people such as procrastination, lack of ambition and their love of comfort, all seem to hinder their progress.

XIX. EARTHS THINK OF THEMSELVES AS PEOPLE WHO LIVE BY REASON ALONE, YET EMOTIONS PLAY AN IMPORTANT ROLE IN HOW THEY NAVIGATE THROUGH LIFE.

This point is very important. Most Earth people think of themselves as not being overly emotional in their behavior. This is because they compare themselves to the "cry-baby" type found in the tree people, who often gravitate toward the Earths for protection and comfort. However, it is not true that the Earth people are mainly driven by reasoning and calculations, like most of the metal people are. Earths are unique in their capacity for intelligence in two different ways -- one gained through emotional connections with people, the other gained through logic and reason. However because Earths, regardless of their gender, think of themselves as strong people, they associate their ways of thinking with those of the metal people. They realize that although they are probably not as good at it as metals, they still refuse to acknowledge this is due to a big portion of their knowledge coming from their emotional bonds created with others.

XX. EARTHS ARE "COMFORT CREATURES."

They do not like to get up particularly early and yet they will not sleep past noon (like waters do) because they don't want to miss good breakfast and other desirable activities happening in the house between 9 and 11 o'clock. Earths like to wear nice clothes and look good, but if looking fashionable requires making one's body feel uncomfortable, quizzed or pinched in some way, then, forget about it! Being relaxed and comfortable all the time is the ultimate agenda of the Strong-Earth person. "Chill out," is addressed by the Earths to the fiery and metallic environment of modern successful people and is exactly how most Earths feel about life. Nothing can be exciting enough to propel a true earth person into action if they sit in front of a TV watching their favorite movie with a good friend. And if you add a cup of hot chocolate or a bag of potato chips the world becomes a perfect place indeed!

Summary on the Characteristics of the 5-Elements

Now that you have read through the natural characteristics of Fire, Water, Tree, Metal and Earth behavior, you can decide which element you are. If you share at least half of a particular element's traits you definitely experience that element's influence on your life. If nearly all characteristics of a particular element are true for you, this means you are completely ruled by it. For most people, there are second, even third elements. For the purposes of self-cultivation and learning how to preserve and increase the supply of your personal Qi, it is useful to create a rough map of your elements. For example, one of my friends identifies herself as 80% water and 20% earth. Another friend sees himself as 60% tree, 20% fire and 20% metal. Yet another visualizes herself as 65% fire and 35% metal. I recommend that you create your own symbolic chart of your 5-element ratios. Mathematic precision is not as important here (unless you are a metal ☺). Just remember that your elemental composition will change several times during your life cycle as discussed in the next chapter.

Further on we will be discussing more practical uses for knowing your own elements, such as the energy boosters. Each element has particular things that boost its energy or deplete its energy. Finding out what elements you are dominant in can help to increase your wellbeing and personal Qi. It can also improve the way you relate to other elements in daily life interactions.

When reading the descriptions of each element it is important to understand that we are not intending to give people "labels or stereotypes". Knowing which elements we are helps us see our true nature for what it really is and hopefully bring more happiness and fulfillment into our life.

Chapter Six

How 5-Elements Change During a Lifetime

Composition of your natural Qi, in terms of the 5-Elements, will change several times throughout your life time. Getting married to a person with the opposite element (such as fire marrying water, or tree marrying metal) will definitely change you. Giving birth to a child whose element is opposing your own (fire parent and water child, or tree parent and metal child) will also result in sensible alterations to one's natural bio-rhythms.

Other strong factors which profoundly change one's innate Qi-composition are jobs, climates, and food. I will discuss these factors later in Part II where I present information about the energy-boosters for all five elements. In this chapter, we will discuss how we, as human beings, experience all the elements God has created for us by travelling throughout our life's stages and growing mature in our biological age.

There are several different traditions describing the effects of the 5-elements on human life-cycles, but in this book, we introduce only one such tradition, because it is the easiest for the Westerners and Americans to understand and apply to their lives. According to this tradition, we spend approximately twelve years (plus or minus two to three years depending on an individual) under the influence of one element. Between one and twelve years of age - we experience the influence of the tree energy; between twelve and twenty four -- energy of fire; between twenty four and thirty six – energy of Earth; between thirty six and forty eight – energy of metal; and between forty eight and sixty –

energy of water. And then the cycle returns to the Tree element to repeating itself a second time.

Let me explain to you how it works in greater detail. Our human evolution begins with us all experiencing the power of the tree element during the first twelve years of our life. This means as children of that age, we act as the Tree-people in response to many of our life's situations regardless of what our natural element is. In addition to our fiery behavior, if we are born as fires, or our watery behavior, if we are born as waters or metal behavior if we are born metals, we all act like Tree-energy just because we are younger than twelve. As one unmistakably notices the difference between a restless, boldly acting girl, who is fire, and quiet, secretive boy, who is water, one can also see that both children, despite the differences in their innate characters, often act with sweetness and kindness characteristic of the tree element in childhood.

All forms of the tree element behavior including messy rooms, inability to lie, failure to be on time, and so forth are naturally exhibited in children of that age. But in people innately endowed by other elements, these traits disappear replaced with the metallic, fiery, watery or earthy attributes, with only the innate trees retaining their qualities as adults.

Human societies have recognized this particular tree-energy of children, often wishing to access it for adult gain. This is why communication with children is sometimes considered to be therapeutic and even divine in so many cultures around the world. For example, in the Catholic Church, the altar boys were and are often selected from this particular age group, and the Gregorian chant was traditionally performed by boys who have not reached puberty. Flower-girls for wedding ceremonies were and are traditionally selected from girls before the age of puberty.

Kids naturally embody the spontaneous carefree tree energy

The angelic, divine, selfless energy similar to beautiful flowers and trees that flows abundantly in young children is the center of attention in many cultures where this energy is often used during special religious or spiritual practices. However, few traditions explain how this abundant tree-energy can be easily destroyed. This is why the knowledge of the 5-elements may be so useful to us, so that we can avoid destroying it preciousness.

The 5-elements theory teaches that, because the innate gentleness and beauty of the tree energy during the ages of one through twelve is so active and revealed to everyone, it can be abused and destroyed if not properly protected. For instance, one must be aware that a child's sweetness can be easily burned by an adult with too much fire Qi; or it can be unconsciously hacked, cut down and mutilated by an adult who indulges in her or his metal Qi power. As a result, the sweetness of the tree will disappear in a child before it is time. Depending on how the tree energy had been injured or brutalized, we may end up creating a young person whose internal energy portrait looks like a bare tree-trunk without branches or leaves, a stump, or something burned to ashes, covered in cold black coals – these internal archetypes will serve as foundations for a miserably horrific, adult character. 5-elements theory explains how people with sadistic, criminal inclinations result from the destruction of their early childhood sweet tree energy by adults in their life.

In Asia, both the Daoist and Confucian scholars paid a great deal of attention to the innate energies of a child in order to preserve their natural Qi. They also maintained the awareness that compassionate, kind and sensitive behavior is most easily taught to people younger than twelve. This is why their education required all children under twelve be trained in the virtue of the Xiao. Xiao is based on the natural kind of love children and parents have for each other.

It requires remembering daily the sensation of sweet loving and caring for one's mother, father, sisters and brothers, and then, consciously expanding this sensation to distant relatives, then, to all people related to your family, then, to all people who live in the same country, and then, to all people. I find this a most beautiful exercise, teaching children (and adults) how to love others in an easy, natural way.

It is time for us to move on to the next twelve years of human life. It comes, more or less, between the years of twelve and twenty four. During this phase, we all experience the power of fire. Once again, this occurs regardless of what our innate element is. We all feel and act like fire if our age is somewhere between twelve and twenty-four. Of course, if one's natural Qi *is* fire, the degree of the crazy burning and testing everyone's patience during these years will be enormous. At the same time, for an innate water person the fiery earnings, blasting disrespectfulness, and internal itching for something new will still affect this person's life, but will be less than what the fire or tree people experience. For the trees, this age is a particularly dangerous time. Parents who have the tree-children, please, beware. This is the time when they are burned one way or another, so parental supervision during their first romantic involvement is highly advised.

The fire phase of life is mainly about discovering the power of romantic love for another person, as well as the power of our sexual desires, which run over our ability to think or control our own behavior. Sexual energy, in many cultural expressions such as poetry and singing, is associated with an irresistible desire to burn and melt with someone else's energy, to create one energy-field and one living entity out of parts that exist separately and independently of each other. It is also naturally associated with destroying and clearing away all obstacles that prevent such merging.

High school is notoriously ruled by the fire archetype

This is why most people display their fire-Qi during erotic experiences beginning at twelve to thirteen years of age. By the time we are eighteen years old, our sexual powers have reached their strongest and desires may seem almost insatiable. I always tell my students, who complain about their hearts being broken by love, that as they grow older they will never get to experience the burning of love in the same way they enjoy it now, therefore -- stop complaining! Yes, we will still be able to love and enjoy strong sexual impulses toward our loved ones, but never again will our passions reach the Himalayan heights of the fire-phase burning. After all, during that time our business is "destroying" the entire supply of the tree-energy, which we saved up during the first twelve years of our lives ☺.

This crazy, almost complete preoccupation with sexual activities phase does fade away, and is replaced with the Earth energy. Under its influence, between the ages of twenty-four and thirty-six, we are given a chance to recuperate, count the damage and reconstruct our lives. I have not found many human beings who were not "burned" by love between the ages of twelve and twenty-four. And this is why it is wise to begin looking for grounding of some sort beginning on our twenty fifth or twenty sixth birthday.

The influence of the Earth-Qi is neutral, constructive and relatively slow. Parents of children that age may finally begin feeling better about their offspring, realizing that they somehow, almost miraculously, adjusted to this world and will ultimately survive, even prosper. They were not so sure of that before, when the fire-phase was testing and torturing them. Fire can be a time when people go to jail, commit all sorts of unintended crimes, get into car accidents, or truly hate their own parents.

During the Earth phase however, people settle down. This is the best phase to buy property, invest money and time

Fire decreases and Earth becomes stronger after kids arrive

into important projects, marry, have children, and act on other life-interests. If I were a minister of education, I would decree that people between the ages of twelve and twenty four be allowed to go nuts, simultaneously be taught about the nature of romantic love and relationships, travel as much as possible and be given plenty of time to commune with the nature and its wild creatures. I would not keep them in college classrooms, because this is the same as trying to keep fire in a wooden box. When people are in the phase of fire they are going to act crazy no matter what! I would start giving people serious professional education around the time they turn twenty four or twenty five when, due to the natural circulation of Qi, the Earth energy begins to rise in their character. This is because at this age, people finally become very interested in acquiring things of all sorts, including knowledge. They all want to feel solid about their lives in response to the Earth-element vibrations as they begin to work on their physical bodies and their spiritual minds.

Most people intuitively recognize the Earth-energy calling for material abundance and create some form of prosperous, solid household in one form or another. After that however, a difficult time may come. Roughly between the ages of thirty-six and forty-eight (could be a bit earlier or later for some people), the metal phase comes in. Around this time life is difficult for almost all people, even if they are metals themselves. In our society we call this a mid-life crisis. The key to doing your absolute best with these twelve years starts with understanding the nature of the metal-Qi vibrations. The rising of the metal energy forces us to evaluate, very critically everything that we and other people have done during our lives up to this point. We evaluate, even become critical of our marriage or long-term romantic engagements. If we don't have either of these, we become very critical of our short term engagements. Whatever we do

Metal stages of life often bring life-evaluation and silver hair

as a way of expressing our love for another person may be subjected to some form of rather unpleasant scrutiny during this time. Worst of all, it can eat us from within consistently, for nearly a decade. This would be the time to decide – are you staying with the same partner? If yes, then why? Or – are you going to finally divorce the person who has been holding you back from accomplishing the multitudes of amazing things you have come here to accomplish? And if yes, how are you going to do it?

Seriously worrying about all the important financial issues, such as properties, investments, retirements, pensions, medical plans, the same problems affecting our loved ones, will fall roughly on this decade, because it is ruled by metal. (Note: For some fires and trees its affects might be delayed a bit, meaning they would begin thinking about these things by their later forties, but may not act "metallically" on them until they turn fifty).

If one was born a natural metal, this phase may be extremely painful. But if one's innate Qi is water, it will be relatively easy, because metal supports water. In fact, for the quiet, barely noticeable people born with the innate Qi of water, the metal phase can be very pleasant. It can turn out to be the only time when people around them finally notice their wonderful, peaceful and supportive personalities. It can be the only time when they finally get a promotion they had been deprived of all these years. Some unexpected money may come their way, seemingly out of nowhere. Or they may meet someone who will provide them with stability, allowing the return of a more enjoyable life and some rejuvenation.

Regardless of the type of one's natural Qi, most people during the Metal phase (thirty-six to forty-eight) develop a strong sense of what they want from their lives, as well as a general feeling for what is right or wrong specifically for them. In a funny kind of way, this is also the phase when many people completely reverse beliefs they have always held. For example, liberals become more conservative, and conservatives more liberal. Some people become more religious even if they have not been known to have any interest in religion before. Others can all of the sudden give up their burning religious passions and their faith acquires a quieter, more peaceful nature.

The metal phase in our lives is the time when everything that we believed to be true and to exist in a certain way is going to be subjected to a very serious test by our own critical abilities, and subsequently, all things that mattered to us will be confirmed as truth or dismissed as a folly. As the main functions of the Metal-Qi are rational thinking, critical evaluation, judging, organizing, selecting the "good" and discarding the "bad" – none of us will escape doing these as we enter our thirties and move into our forties.

After the Metal phase is over (many may think like I did, that it will never end, but it will! Believe me!) there will come the phase ruled by the energy of the water. This occurs between the ages of forty-eight and sixty. For some people, this may be the easiest time of their lives, such as those who receive an early retirement. Yet, for others the water phase may be experienced as more difficult than the metal phase. Fire especially may be tested the most, unless they are prepared by the knowledge of how our bio-magnetic fields change according to the 5-elements theory. For the fires, this time can bring on the greatest pain and disappointment, because this is the phase when all the natural craziness of the younger years disappears entirely. Fires do not like to feel quiet. Fires have a hard time understanding the concept of aging. In addition to this challenge, the water phase may be experienced as a time when their past comes to haunt them in an unusual and even mysterious way. Maybe it is the unexpected return into their lives of a former "enemy-person" whom they have not seen for twenty years or longer. It can be also the return of a disease they had as very young people, which did not bother them for nearly twenty years but now it is back, worse than before. It can also be a time for them to develop a disease, which doctors cannot diagnose because it is a cumulative result of so many years and so many types of reckless behaviors. In other words, unless the fires gain wisdom, arriving prepared spiritually, emotionally and intellectually, they may experience this phase of the water as a personal tragedy.

One of my friends wrote to me once telling me she could not be fire anymore, but that without being fire, she does not feel she is the same person. This basically sums up the challenge of fire-personality during the water phase of life. Most of our celebrities are the fire-archetype. They have lots of money and they use it to trick the natural cycles of their Qi. They try to preserve fire energy artificially through the use of hormones, drugs and through scandalous, teenage-like behavior, as well as expensive, painful surgeries removing all traces of age from their faces and bodies. However, it does not work. And you can easily observe for yourself that the fire-celebrities whose performances you highly enjoyed while they were young and in their natural fire-phase are no longer interesting and appealing to you unless they somehow changed once they reached the watery phase of their life. The celebrities who we are still entertained by and excited to watch are those who added water-Qi to their performance repertoire, and thus grew successfully in wisdom and now possess new knowledge to offer to all of us. Quite often, such transformation occurs for these celebrities as a result of a near-death experience or another strong experience, which nearly sent their fire Qi to

Water years bring wisdom - helping us see the big picture
After age 60 we reenter the cycle as tree again
to become child-like once more

be extinguished. Once they find a way to bring fire back, its nature is changed more like "light" rather than burning fire.

The tree people usually age gracefully and do relatively well during the phase of water. They easily embrace the loss of the younger traits in their looks and behavior and do not regret the loss of youthful aggressiveness. They do not mind becoming child-like again. This is why the trees make wonderful grand-parents and can continue successfully in the service and care-giving professions they chose for themselves such as, advisors, teachers, nurses and sale-persons. Metals do relatively well during the water phase, because they have already prepared a comfortable retirement plan for themselves and their spouses, and planned all other "important" things for the old age. They continue being methodical and pedantic through their aging, which may irritate the non-metal people with whom they have a relationship. Yet, the good news is as the water-phase progresses, it usually rusts away the sharp, unpleasant edges of the metal personality. As a result they may appear nicer, softer, more pleasant and less judgmental during this time. The danger of course is that sometimes, in order to balance the metals' extremely rational behavior they exhibit most of their lives, the water phase may bring on some form of dementia or Alzheimer's disease. From what I have observed, it is people with the innate power of the metal Qi who get these conditions more often than people whose lives have been affected by other elements.

The water-phase helps us acquire wisdom, become more calm, content, and forgiving. In this respect, I say much needs to be done in our society in order to embrace the natural, graceful rhythms of the water energy visiting us in our mature age. *In our culture the fire and the metal archetypes are the most popular, since we view them as the most successful examples of human life.* So we tend to impose forms of behavior associated with the fire and metal archetypes on all phases of our lives, regardless of where we are in our personal evolution. For example, we think that it's good for someone to be approaching the end of life and still act like a teenager. We do not value the quiet, meditative, self-absorbed traits which come naturally to us, as we stay longer and longer in this God-given life. Our culture almost demands that we keep ourselves busy and remain loud participants in the same forms of activities we have been busy with our entire life. When people, under the influence of the water phase, become quieter, more pensive, and withdrawn, it scares us. We do not view this as a beautiful, necessary preparation for departure from this planet and return to God. Instead, we panic as we see the change in our loved ones' behavior and because fear that slowing down leads them to their death, we force them to stay engaged in what seems to them, vanities of life. But death and the ultimate quiet time are approaching whether we want them or not! According to the wisdom of many traditions, including that of the 5-elements, there must be time for everything, therefore, there must be time for us to become pensive, self-reflective, yielding and humble, and allow others to enjoy their entrance into this stage. In order to fully embrace the water-phase's vibrations in our lives, we are advised to: Consume less, talk less, get rid of most possessions, think less about ourselves, buy only bare necessities (we don't need all this stuff when we go), and spend more time with friends, family, nature and animals. These are the messages of the water-Qi, and I wish more of us would listen to them, because that can make such a change in our society!

Now, what happens to us after we become humble and selfless during the water phase as we think about and prepare for the departure from this planet? According to the concept of the 5-elements, if we accept the quieting of our life-vibrations, we can consolidate enough energy for the next sixty-year cycle. If we deliberately pause during the water-Qi phase, it can purify, calm and renew our bio-magnetic field, then, we can go back to experiencing the tree energy again. It will be followed by the new phases of fire, Earth, metal and then the second water phase, which total the number of years we can spend in this physical body on Earth, to one hundred and twenty. This is now becoming an accepted, scientific medical view on human physiology. More doctors now believe we can easily live up to a hundred years old or more, if we conduct ourselves wisely, living according to the laws nature, which 5-elements speak of. Even the old testament Genesis chapter 6 verse 3 tells us, *"And the LORD said, My spirit shall not always strive with man, for that he also is flesh: yet his days shall be an hundred and twenty years."*

During the return of the tree-phase in modern America, we often observe people developing a strong sense of compassion, kindness, and desire to care for other human beings and creatures of nature. Their rescue missions and operations sometimes, in fact, grew more successful during their second tree-phase (sixty and older). Jane Goodal's mission to save the chimpanzees is a perfect example of a successful, strong return of the tree phase. So is the story of mother Teresa and many others who were truly able to draw themselves closer to God and the eternal life during the older years of their lives.

In other cases, during the second return of the tree phase we encounter people who loose control over their lives, becoming dependent on others for their survival. In a sense, being like children again, for yet again they must trust other people's mercy for everything, even a trip to the bathroom or getting food into the mouth.

From sixty to seventy-two, the second return of the tree phase is going to affect us depending on how we are prepared to face it. After that, the second phase of fire returns. If you have ever met a man or woman in their mid-seventies full of passion, in fact, more passionate than any young person you've ever met; you have encountered a human experiencing their second fire phase. This is something to behold! I had the privilege to observe my Chinese teacher in this stage. I also met a female Shaman who was seventy-five and stronger in spirit than all of my students put together. Biographies of Daoist and Buddhist monks in the Tibetan and Chinese traditions where the knowledge of the 5-elements was common give us a colorful description of what life might be during the second phase of fire, provided we have rested during the previous water stage and were able to renew ourselves during the precious phase of the tree.

Great human beings during the second phase of fire turn themselves into a source of the divine light. They reach the point where they surrender to God unconditionally. The entire ego is burned by this point in the game. All human tragedies have been played out. By the time we reach our seventies we have basically seen everything we need to see to know what it means to be human. And we've seen the work of the divine wisdom in its full display. The people alive and wise after their mid-seventies do not waste any time on unimportant preoccupations. They do not gossip, do not accumulate possessions, do not get angry, they eat very little and sleep very little too. All the time they have is used to serve the divine truth and reconnect as many human beings as possible back to their Creator. This is the main idea behind us being allowed to stay here living longer lives. Of course, many do not chose to transform into the light during this time and still act out of selfish, carnal desires.

Chapter Seven

Why the Zodiac is Often Not Accurate

I told you according to my research, the 5-Element system works much more efficiently when people decide for themselves what their first, second and third elements are. I mentioned this makes our method of application of the 5-element theory unique, because if you were to learn it from an Asian teacher, your elements would be decided on the basis of the year and hour of your birth. And most likely, you would not find this information to be useful and conclude that this system does not work for you.

First, let us look at how you can find your innate element in accordance with the *traditional* Asian system of zodiacs, without breaking your brain. You can do it using the last digit of the year of your birth. Then, I will explain to you why – after you find out what element you are according to the traditional system -- you most likely are going to feel that it does not make sense to you, at the same time, you have probably felt that the previous chapters described you and everyone you know in your life nearly perfectly.

So, let us get to the calculations. Look at the last digit of your birth-year. If it is 0 or 1 you are considered to be born under the influence of the metal Qi. If it is 2 or 3, you are born under the influence of Qi of water. If it is 4 or 5, you are influenced by the Qi of the tree. If it is 6 or 7 you are influenced by the Qi of fire. And, if it is 8 or 9, you are influenced by the Qi of Earth.

If you are born close to the beginning of the year, your energy is traditionally believed to be the continuation of the previous year's element, because the Asian zodiac switches gears when the Asian New Year begins, in early

February. So, for instance, if someone is born on January 10 of 1988 that person's element is not the Earth, but Fire because the Fire energy of 1987 is still active in January.

However, you do not have to worry about learning all these complexities of the Asian system of zodiac, and it is not my goal to teach it to you. I am *not* teaching it to you as most Westerners benefit from the knowledge of the 5-Elements differently than people from Asian countries. I would like to add that Westerners, including Americans, benefit from the 5-elements knowledge despite the fact that when they find out what their element is (according to the Asian birth year tradition) they usually shake their heads and say that it absolutely makes no sense to them. The main reason the traditional Asian system makes no sense to us is that in our societies, the innate Qi that we are born with is for the most part destroyed through family and school education. And this is why I always ask my students, as I do ask you, to identify the first, second and third element that you think is active in your life solely on the basis of your current personality and actual behavior. Why this is the most useful way for us, becomes clear after you read this statement from one of my students, John, who was born a fire (birth year ending in a six or seven), but was forced into water-behavior by his parents:

"When I did the test with Professor Storch I thought I was water, because I am always quiet, don't like to talk to people and prefer to keep to myself, but then she told me about the traditional way of finding one's element by looking at the last digit of my year of birth. By this system, I found out that I was born on the year of the "fire tiger" and therefore my innate element must be fire. I was shocked and decided to ask my parents if I ever exhibited the fire-kind of behavior as a child. And they said, 'Oh, yes! Yes, of course! This is why we had to put you on medication very early because you

128

never listened to anyone and always got yourself into trouble. No babysitter would ever come to stay with you. They were actually afraid of you when you were only three years old, can you believe it?'

Then I understood what happened. My innate Qi of fire was so unacceptable for my family that they had to totally suppress it, and I developed the water energy early on due to medication and because I felt depressed all the time. Now come to think about my profession – I am a Firefighter, but when I am taking down the flames I sometimes feel like crying. I had no idea why I was so weird that way. But now it all makes sense to me."

In contrast, Asian countries such as Vietnam, Korea, Japan or China, the great usefulness of the 5-elements system has been known for thousands of years. As a result, Asian parents, for the most part, avoid random pregnancies instead choosing the type of Qi they need to add to their families through birth of a new child in order to maintain overall balance, peace and continue with the family business and reputation.

Although it is difficult for us to believe, ten to eleven months before the element Earth begins to rise, especially if the Earth is in the shape of a dragon, all the contraceptive businesses across Asia close down, because married couples try their best to conceive a child during that time. By the same token, if the years of fire are approaching, especially if fire is in a form of tiger, the contraceptive businesses become very profitable, because no one wants to have a child with the potential to destroy the entire family and its fortunes.

In the West, we usually think about such cultural behavior in a condescending way, calling it superstitions, but let me ask you; have you not observed for yourself how absolutely respectful Asian children are of their parents and families in general? If you ask me, paying attention to how natural forces work and not thinking that we are above them speaks of wisdom, not superstitions.

In most Asian families, people are well aware of what element their future child is going to be and for this reason they are prepared to deal with their element instead of destroy it. But it is not so in our culture. And I want to share with you two more statements written by students who studied 5-elements with me at the University of Florida and University of the Pacific.

The first story is Alina's. She was born as a Tree person. Everybody remembered her as the sweetest child as can be, with many calling her "little angel." However, she was molested by her uncle when she was ten, and with this crime, the sweetness of her character was gone forever. It was replaced by metal. Alina wrote that as a young adult, she could not stand the display of emotions, any kind of emotions, except justified anger. She enjoyed being busy and working hard to save more and more money for her future. In relationships she enjoyed being victorious and independent and always selected men who were of the tree nature, because it was so easy to boss them around. When she studied the 5-elements she was surprised by that she felt drawn to so many tree characteristics despite the fact she did not act like that in her real life. At first she thought this was because her current boy-friend was a typical tree-person. Then slowly she realized she would like to be a kind, nice person again, but was afraid to, because if she were to become nice again, she would be defenseless and something bad could happen to her again.

The second story is of a young man Josh who acted like a typical water-archetype when he was a child. However at age fourteen, Josh decided to become a missionary. When he arrived in Africa he realized that no matter what he did or said, people paid him no attention. Then one of the village people told Josh that he must learn how to speak the "African way," meaning, using a loud voice, speaking very passionately, almost screaming with enthusiasm of his faith. Josh said this was a single most difficult thing he had to do in his life – to change his innate character in order for his mission to be successful, but he did it. When he wrote about his training with the 5-elements, he said that he was able to accomplish something that few masters could do – be at home with the fire and water energies simultaneously.

We can conclude this chapter by briefly addressing parents. Please, please, pay very close attention to the natural bio-magnetic vibrations of your child's character. Let the fires be the fires no matter how difficult it may seem, of course, providing all the necessary safeguards for them and yourself. Do not give children pills just because their behavior is so fiery and they are unruly, very loud or never sit still. Teach them how to respect your rules by using the power of metal (instant cause and effect rule enforcement) and water (patience and not overreacting to outbursts), but do not kill their innate vibrations of fire. Disciplining our fiery children with metal and water can provide the greatest support system for our children's health, happiness and social success.

Parents of children with extremely watery behavior, you have no reasons to worry. Allow your child to have all the quiet and lonely time she or he needs in order to be themselves. But then help them discover their tree, metal and fire energies, but do it gently and slowly without pushing, scaring or provoking the water-child. The worst thing a parent can do to confront watery behavior in a little person is to call them a chicken and push them into a lake to teach them how to swim. This will work perfectly for a

Kids with strong fire Qi may rebel against tree parents
They are balanced with metal and water archetypes

fire-child and usually it is a fire-parent who likes to use this technique on her or his children thinking that they just need to be sufficiently challenged and that's all. But it is not. The water-child's psychology and physiological responses are entirely different from those of the fire-parent. There is no use in forcing them into action. One must simply wait. And since waiting is the most difficult thing for the fire-person to do, we must conclude that water-children are born to fire-parents to teach them important lessons about balancing our Qi.

Children must be observed by parents very carefully to understand how they *naturally* respond to situations. Are they: Becoming bossy and judgmental? Sweet talking you into buying what they want? Fighting, no matter what, not actually caring about the results? Happiest when left alone? Or do they possess the kind of character Asian parents prefer; a little bit of everything?

In the following chapters I am going to discuss the energy-boosters for the 5-elements. These boosters are good for adults, but can also be used for children, with some modifications of course. The goal is to become the most of what we can be according to our God's most generous plan for us and our innate talents.

PART II

Energy Boosters for the 5-Elements

According to my teacher (and more than twenty years experience teaching this 5-element system to students) we can increase our present supply of life force, or Qi, by regularly practicing three things: 1.Consciously connecting to our own elements. 2. Avoiding injuries from the elements which oppose our own. 3. Developing additional elements in our character, which we learn how to do by allowing support and giving support to all life forms.

In the following five chapters, we share with you ancient wisdom on how to consciously connect to your own element by (A) using the healing colors (B) eating and drinking that which are most supportive to your element (C) planning things around the time of the year and hours of the day which give the highest support to your natural elements (D) staying in geographic locations where climate and weather support your Qi (E) paying special attention to organ-systems in your body that your element needs most.

Chapter Eight

Energy Boosters for the Fire-People

All shades of bright orange, red and yellow always support the fire people, because these colors invigorate their internal flame. Therefore, fire people will always feel better when surrounded by these colors. So, my dear fire-people, wear red, orange, gold and yellow as often as you can -- and you will notice a positive change in your daily energy levels!

Additionally, fires can post objects using these colors like using pieces of fabric, jewels or artwork, on their living room or office walls. If you are a real fire, you can try them in your bedroom! One of my fire friends sleeps on silky red sheets and pillows in the spring and under a fuzzy maroon comforter in the winter and she loves it!

Please, notice that "fires" who have been deeply wounded and lost lots of their energy, have a tendency toward switching from bright colors to black. This represents their "flame reduced to cold coals" condition of their life force, which requires immediate attention.

Fire energy booster foods are anything with a hot temperature, such as; tea, coffee, soup, porridge or stew. Spicy-hot foods such as; chili peppers, cinnamon or curry are great boosters too. Fire people are also turned on, and energy empowered mightily by everything new and exotic. If you are a fire person, eating the same food for three days will kill you! So, invent new, exciting combinations of foods and drinks every time you prepare a meal. This will make you feel very powerful!

The most favorable time of the year for the fire person is summer. This is the time when they should jumpstart their most important projects, such as moving to a new location, getting a new job, finding a mate, or creating a new circle of friends. Fire elements should have plenty of sun and outdoor activities during summer and through the entire year. Otherwise, in the absence of their beloved source of energy, the sun, they feel week and depressed.

Fire people also like being naked, which goes well with their love of warmth and dry heat. If you are with the fire partner, you need to know that your lover longs for a life without clothes. And yes, the fire people's energy is going to be boosted if they allow themselves to stay and move around naked, or better yet, if they dance naked to some fiery tune right before they get out of the house.

In terms of the hours of the day that give fire people most of their energy, it is, of course, noon time. Fires feel their strongest then because they are supported by the daily cycle of the sun as it reaches its highest point on the horizon around noon. For this reason, fire people usually enjoy lunch (or brunch) as the best meal of the day, and they should stick with it! Being a fire myself, I know that we do not care much about our breakfast (unlike the tree-people who cannot start their day without eating their very "special breakfast"), but by eleven or twelve o'clock we become ravenously hungry and if we don't eat right away we can eat someone else instead.

Noon is not merely the time "fires" prefer to eat most of their food. Noon is also a time they can be hungry sexually. Fires, in fact, may prefer to make love around noon (or early afternoon) rather than late evening, because fires exert themselves during the day and their energy level may go down toward the evening, leaving them with no sexual drive. For most "fires," noon is also prime time for physical exercises, making important decisions and sending important messages.

136

Fire people love the sun and prosper in Southern climates

In terms of geographic locations, "fires" are associated with the energy of the south, and in my observation, they do much better in the warm Southern climate than in any other. If you live in the United States and you are fire, you are going to feel miserable in Minnesota or North Dakota no matter how much money you make, how much you love your job or your family. For fires, best locations are found in New Mexico, Arizona, California, Utah, Georgia, Carolinas, Florida, or other similar climate conditions. Fires, however, must be aware that high humidity (which is water element) has a strong potential to destroy their life force unless they develop significant presence of the water element in their character. Georgia and Florida nearly destroyed the life and health of several fire people I know, yet, numerous Yoga, Reiki and Qigong instructors whose innate fire element is balanced by cultivated water element are doing very well there. When people reach the age of fifty and beyond the water element naturally develops in their bio-magnetic field. This is why most retired people, regardless of their innate element, are doing well in the Florida climate.

To maximize the fire-peoples' creativity, it is best for them not only move to the south-influenced states or countries, but also to settle in the south-influenced residences and work places. Fire people are advised to maintain free access to the southern, sunny walls of the houses and sit there during the colder days of winter. The southern area of their yard or garden must be made easily accessible, as well, and used regularly for outdoor activities. Hammocks and circle-shaped seating can be located there and at least one window in the house must face southward. Residences of the fire people, in general, would be best oriented toward south, south-east or south-west. They would be wise to be careful about avoiding places with the "northern influences."

The internal organ that is supportive of the fire Qi is the heart. It makes sense that people who enjoy living their lives to the fullest, spend lots of time in the sun, risk their lives, and eat hot, spicy food, should rely heavily on the function of their heart and for this reason all fires must pay special attention to the health of their hearts, no matter how young or old they may be. Fire people are advised to start a spiritual practice of connecting their lives to their heart. This includes thanking it for all the amazing work this organ is doing for them. If they are at risk for heart disease, Reishi mushroom and following the protocol for heart disease in the "Conquering Any Disease" book can be very helpful. It lists all the foods that have reversed heart disease and high cholesterol for thousands of people. Many fires have exhausted their heart Qi by burning the candle at both ends. Therefore, in addition to the fires learning the ways of water (energy conservation and patience), it is imperative for them to adopt a more heart friendly diet. This is not the same diet that most people "think" is heart healthy, so please reference the book above for accurate and specific details.

My Daoist teacher taught me a practice called "cooling the heart", because he knew I was dominated by fire Qi. The practice includes several very simple and efficient techniques: 1. Keep the upper part of your body undressed often as possible (given it doesn't disturb others) 2. Place your left hand, palm down, on a cold surface such as metal or ice, and hold it there for five or so minutes. Repeat until you can physically feel the calming of your heart. 3. Hold in your left hand a silver ball while concentrating on the heart, asking it to cool down and relax. 4. While doing Nine-Breath Method Qigong, designed by Jeff Primack, try to slow your breathing down to 2 breaths a minute or slower.

Chapter Nine

Energy Boosters for the Water People

All shades of blue support the water-people's energy. These colors' vibrations are similar to that of lakes, rivers, oceans and rain. This is why they make the water-people happy. Well, water people do not really show their happiness that much. I mean, not like the fire or tree people do. I think it serves us well to remember that it will be a waste of energy to try to make a water-person *show* their happiness for us. When waters are happy, they appear content, and this is good enough. In fact, it is dangerous for a water-person to switch to a fiery, ecstatic emotional state. This is why waters must surround themselves with the "blue energies."

I will note here that for most of us, green and blue colors are very close, but this is not so for the water-people. Unless they also have the tree element, they do not like green colors on their bodies. They are ok with green in their surroundings, but not directly on them. So here is advice for you -- do not waste your money on buying a pair of green pants or green jacket for your water family member or friend. If you wish to please him or her, carefully observe what they wear, and you will see a "particular shade of blue" that they favor above all other blues. Then, buy things for them which come in this particular blue color. The magic of a water personality is; *they never get tired of the same things.*

Food for the water-people is more of necessity than a celebration of life (therein lies a crucial difference between the "fires" and "waters"). Waters, definitely, *do not see* meals as a wonderful opportunity to get together, to be loud, to party. They prefer to eat alone or in a small, quiet group. They also have the potential to irritate many of us, by being very slow, picky eaters, and by eating as if they do not enjoy their food. Because they enjoy food less than people with other elements, "waters" must do something else while they eat, such as; listen to the radio, watch TV, search for something on a computer, read a book or magazine, stare away from the food towards the other person at the table, through a nearby window or something else of that sort.

One may viably say waters are picky eaters. Some of them refuse to eat certain simple, healthy food such as eggs, celery, tomatoes, onions, cucumbers etc. For each water personality, there exists a list of foods they won't not eat, no matter what. This sort of aversion to certain perfectly good foods is always unpredictable and unexplainable for people with other elements. And as a fire who is married to water, I must say it can be very irritating, because every time I cook I must remember that steamed carrots cannot be added to a stew, or fresh celery cannot be used in a Greek salad, and so on. On the other hand, water-people usually find a dish, or two, which they *really* enjoy and they will stick with this choice for a long, long time.

Water-people's energy is believed to be supported by modest consumption of salty, bitter tasting foods and drinks. Americans for the most part, do not enjoy bitter taste, yet waters find just what they need in dark, bitter beers or by taking their yerba mate without honey or sweetener. Water people can also be fond of cabbage or radish, both of which can have bitter taste. More cultivated waters like to drink bitter herbal teas.

Waters both need and love salt because salt supports what the Chinese call "kidney function." Although excessive consumption of salt can result in kidney stones according to published studies, salty foods (especially those made with pink Himalayan salt) are good for the waters because it makes them feel more energetic. They also need some salt to be added to their dishes because their sense of taste is not as strong as that of people with other elements.

Finally, one can easily observe that waters do not enjoy eating and drinking things hot in temperature, and they should follow this intuitive knowledge as one of their best dietary rules. While fires' energy can be restored by a cup of hot tea, a water person's energy can be destroyed by it. Waters should always wait for a drink or food to cool down to just the right temperature for them, before consuming. Staying on a cool side, in general, is a good thing for the waters, but not beyond a certain point where their energy begins to freeze.

The most beneficial time of year for the water-people is winter. They generally fare better when the weather is colder. One of my water friends runs air-conditioning in December and complains it is never cold enough in northern California to wear his nice-looking sweater and leather jacket. Winter also provides water-people with a natural excuse to withdraw, be slow and stay indoors. Since in the winter most people are in hibernation, we feel more affinity with the waters' passive life-style and the water-people begin feeling less different from others.

For this reason, it is recommended if the water person needs to impress someone, she or he should use the power of winter energy to their advantage. Although waters do not like job searches, or searches of any kind, (except on the Internet, which is solely for their entertainment) winter is their best time to apply for a new position or promotion. Waters are more likely to be successful when they act during the winter months than during the summer.

For the water people to stay healthy, they must live in a climate which is not too warm. Oregon, Washington, the Northern coast of California, Maine, or Vermont would be

Water people do well in cold climates and like wearing coats

ideal locations for the water person's energy comfort. Late autumn and winter time, with its cold crispy nights and days full of clouds and snow, have positive influence on the water personality, giving them a boost in creativity. Much how water becomes stronger when it freezes, a typical water person finds herself or himself a little bit stronger during the colder months of the year and during the cooler hours of the day. However, when it comes to the frigid cold, it is up to the most extreme fire-people to conquer and thrive in it. "Waters" do not do well when the weather reaches cold arctic degrees and stays cold over a prolonged period of time, because they lack the natural Qi of fire.

The hours which feed the water people's energy most strongly are the night hours. This is also their favorite time to eat a meal. The only time the waters might really enjoy consuming food are a very late dinner or snacks taken around or past midnight, however this is a very bad habit according to Jeff Primack's "Conquering Any Disease" book if they have any digestive problems. Water people often suffer from a slower digestive system, unlike fires, which means they should never eat within 3 hours of going to bed. If they suffer from constipation, they should follow the digestion protocol to help their watery (slow) digestive systems become stronger and more efficient.

Waters can properly be called the "queens and kings of the night", because while dispassionate and visibly disengaged during the day, they undergo a remarkable transformation come night hours. It is during the night the water-people become intense and very interesting for us other elements. They can also become adventurous, exciting, even dangerous! This is because their imagination is fed by the energy of the moon and they gain power after the hum-drum of daily routine is gone and the moon governs over the dark universe. Night is the time when water people almost always win video games, write an amazing story or song, or transform into the most seductive and skillful lover one has ever encountered.

Water-people should be excused from social obligations until 1 P.M. This is my opinion, but our society most likely will not change because of that. For those of you who are in love with the water-person like myself, my advice is; be prepared to see them absent-minded until 1 P.M. and schedule no activities with them until even later. At the same time, be ready to share many sleepless nights with your beloved because *this is the time when they really want you, need you, and are in their best shape!*

Water-people should pay close attention to their night time visions, thoughts and dreams. This is the time their minds are at their best and decisions based on "nightly pondering of the nature of things" usually work well for the water people. For the waters who are self-employed, working in business or arts, the night is a good time for productive work, sending important messages and emails, and even placing telephone calls (provided the your business partners are not asleep). Waters, not very talkative during the day, all of a sudden, wish to talk during the night when their language becomes exquisite and thoughts crystal clear.

In terms of geographic locations, waters are associated with the northern direction. In their homes, they must have a northern window or some other access to the energy of the north. It is good for them to plant on the northern side of their garden, firs, ferns, pines and other cold-loving trees and plants. Big rocks with plenty of moss are also good for them. Water-people may find they are more liked by other people and have a more successful social life if they live in Northern countries such as Finland, Norway, Canada, Siberia, Alaska etc.

The internal organ associated with water element is the kidney. If you are the water energy, it is extremely important for you to pay attention to the health of your kidneys and urinary tract. One of the "disorders," which every water-person knows about, but keeps secret, are young water people suffer from bedwetting. If the water-children had their way, they would be awake and active during the night, and the accidents would not occur. But because the water peoples' cycle of life, due to restrictions imposed by our society, must be restricted by what others believe to be a "natural order," waters rarely get a chance to satisfy their biological needs when they have them. This especially shows in their patterns of urination and defecation. Waters hold off necessary trips to the bathroom, because these happen during the hours when they must be asleep, according to a "normal" schedule. Although, as we already know; their life force is in fact awake and active during the night. As their natural biorhythms are constantly thrown off, they may develop bowel or urinary discountenance, constipations, and other problems related to the clearing of the body's liquid and solid waste. Additionally, waters as very shy people, feel psychologically uncomfortable using unfamiliar bathrooms, especially the ones located in public spaces. So, if a water-person plans on living a long, healthy life, he or she must develop a highly personalized and rather conscious, routine of going to the bathroom to effectively clear waste out of the body. It must be done regularly and under conditions he or she finds to be safe and comfortable. See the "tea ritual" in the Conquering Any Disease book for details.

Water people like to be active during the night when kidneys are doing their work. This must be compensated by providing additional help to the kidneys. Special exercises to accomplish this include; all forms of twisting the body's upper part against the lower part and regular rubbing of the low back area with the palms of both hands. Waters can also greatly assist their kidneys by regularly massaging their feet, (which, in their case, are almost always cold) and taking warm foot-baths in the morning and before they go to sleep. My Daoist teacher recommended after we soak our feet in pleasantly warm water for ten to fifteen minutes, we should quickly splash them with cold water, placing them again into the warm water. Splashing with cold water should conclude every feet-bath procedure, after which feet should be rubbed by a towel and put into comfortable sleepers or socks.

Chapter Ten

Energy Boosters for the Tree People

Green color is known to give energy to people with the tree element, and each tree person knows a particular shade of green they appreciate the most. Just like fires can always boost their energy by connecting to the color red, waters feel increased calm and security when surrounded by the color blue; trees should recognize the power of the green vibrations for their body and soul and use it to strengthen themselves. Wearing green colored clothes, including plants in their place of work and residence, even simply feeling or thinking "green" will always make tree people stronger, and allows them to enjoy their great strength in kindness and compassion, rather than the strength defined by metallic character.

At the same time, I have discovered through my research that gentle pastel colors such as light blue, lavender and pink can also be supportive of the tree element. Light shades of beige or yellow, especially in furry or silky fabric, are experienced by many tree-women and men in touch with their sensitivity as both soothing and energizing. In order to find the particular colors which provide the most support, the tree-person should imagine a beautiful garden, or meadow where all the flowers are in bloom, and then notice which colors they like the most. *All the colors one imagines through this exercise are energy boosters.* The tree people must remind themselves that they possess the richest and most nuanced sense of coloring and painting and can easily become successful artists, internal designers or jewelry makers, working with gems, beads, fabrics, flowers, light stones, and wood. Even if a tree person has another job he or she will be greatly soothed, and their natural kindness greatly strengthened by engaging in these ancient arts of beading, kneading, decorating creating flower arrangements.

In the realm of food, all sweet tastes always make tree-people happy and fill them with creative, spring-like energy. If the tree person is in good health, without any diabetes (as often happens to the trees) a good peach or apple pie, a piece of fine chocolate, a scoop of delicious goji berry macadamia ice cream are all energy friends. However, in this era of 1 in 5 people having pre-diabetes and 30% of American people being obese, tree people should eat only high-quality sweets. At the same time, it is crucial for tree people to receive sweet sensations from other sources. Sometimes the urge to eat sweets in the tree person comes from a lack of "sweetness" in ones romantic or family life.

Everything trees do in life must have sweetness. Maintaining positivity is even more crucial for good health than for people with other elements. So my dear trees, stop feeling guilty and start spending time doing what you really want to do, no matter how silly it may appear in the eyes of people with other elements! Spend more time in nature, learn how to dance with nice partners, rescue animals, garden; doing whatever makes you smile constitutes your energy-booster activity. Whatever takes the smile off your face is an energy-drainer! When the tree people do what they love, sweet tasting food will never become an addiction and they will be physically fit and psychologically happy.

The tree people need everything in their life to taste sweet, and this includes *words*. Tree people need to hear nice, kind, loving and caring words more than people with other elements. Tree people need to realize this because if this need for verbal, emotional sweetness is not satisfied, the tree people will become miserable and possibly ill with depression. Trees must also be aware they may become slaves to people who occasionally say sweet things to them, but do not treat them with overall respect. To ensure they have enough sweet words in their lives, trees may wish to say regular positive affirmations to themselves in front of a mirror and/or record words of love in their own voices and listen to these recordings when feeling low.

Spring is the time of year most supportive to the tree people. It is highly beneficial for the tree people to make their most important moves during spring or early summer. April through June is the ideal time for a tree person to; find their ideal mate; move out of an old house; buy a new car; or change careers. The spring time should be maximized by the tree people. Please know in your heart if you were born with the tree energy, the springtime nature is most favorable, allowing you to accomplish much! If a tree person feels very tired or ill, spring is the ideal time to take a vacation for restoration and overall revitalization.

Also remember to enjoy the spring weather to the fullest, because the summer will soon follow and you the tree person are not going to like the heat. Draw in cool, fresh morning breezes each day of the month of May and spend as much time as you can in the garden, among wild flowers and birds. Enjoy and become part of all the early spring activities happening in plant and animal life. This will make your heart sing with joy.

Morning is the most favorable time of day for those born with the tree element. If allowed to follow their natural biorhythms, the tree people's appreciation of the morning hours becomes very noticeable. They will do well to spend time in a garden or watering plants at this time. Breakfast is usually enjoyed more than any other meal and trees are naturally in a better mood during the first part of the day than in the afternoon. Many of my tree-students suffer from loss of energy in the morning because they stay up late studying

Trees are healed by gardening and waking up at sunrise

or partying, don't get up until it's almost ten o'clock and must rush to their classes. If they get up early without adequate sleep, their morning magic will not appear then either. Some of my tree friends have adjusted their schedule to go bed before 11pm and get up around 6am, which allows them to have their tea, do Qigong or Yoga in the park, drink smoothies or have breakfast mindfully, water plants etc. They report to me that their lives changed dramatically, making them much happier people than they have ever been. Jeff Primack thinks that *everyone* should sleep and wake up at these "tree hours", because it takes advantage of the pineal gland's natural melatonin secretion between 10pm and 2am, which requires we are actually sleeping during these crucial hours. However, I disagree with him on this, because we are all wired differently based on our dominating elements. Waters may feel better staying up late and waking up later. If you work a regular 9am to 5pm job schedule, waking up at sunrise would probably be empowering to give yourself a longer morning for Qigong, smoothies, healthy breakfast etc.

The tree people are the most natural morning people and are therefore advised to stop frequenting parties that go late into the night. Please realize that as a tree person, you are not considered popular at a party running past mid-night. Past mid-night zone is great for the water-people, but not for your fresh, morning gardener, gentle and sweet spirit. Your most enjoyable time for fun ends soon after the sun goes down and if you respect this, returning home before twelve, (just like Cinderella) you will be able to get up reasonably early to either meditate on your porch with a cup of your favorite tea.

Another piece of tree advice; do not let your morning hours evolve into a gigantic, stress-generating machine. If you must take care of other people in the morning, (children, dependent parents, demanding spouses) develop enough metal in the middle of your sweetness and tell them; "Morning is my sacred time! This is when I worship God's glory and tend to the garden of my soul. I must be able to enjoy it in order to be physically and emotionally healthy."

The internal organ symbolically associated with the health of a tree-person is the liver. Liver is responsible for blood cleansing, and providing beautiful silky, shiny skin to the tree people when they are in sound health. But when they abuse their livers through a careless diet, endless stress, grief, or drinking, they may have more skin problems than people who are born under influence of a different element. In my observation, in stressful situations a fire person may have a heart attack, while a tree person will develop a terrible skin rash on their face, hands or entire body. Cancer, especially of the liver also seems to be more prevalent among the kind, gentle and self-sacrificial tree people.

Here is simple advice from my teacher for the trees to maintain happy livers; first, learn how to laugh and smile a lot. Smile and laugh, no matter what, and your liver will be always happy. Second, always drink plenty of herbal teas known to be powerful liver cleansers such as chamomile, mint, rosehip, and dandelion. Three, when practicing breathing techniques and yoga, imagine emerald green light traveling to your liver, keeping it bright and happy. Five, talk to your liver asking it to be happy and thank it for all the work it does to keep your skin beautiful and shiny. Six, through your warm hands send energy by placing them over the liver in front and back, gently massaging the entire area.

Chapter Eleven

Energy Boosters for the Metal People

In ancient China the traditional power-color for the metal people was pure white. I recommend that metal people regularly meditate on the color pure white, plus each time they put on a white dress or t-shirt they think about the color's significance. Its purity, honesty, and integrity will serve as a good reminder of why God gave metals so much power.

I have also discovered that metals are invigorated by colors which create a good contrast. For example, they like to wear white t-shirts and blue jeans, black skirts with red blouses (especially if fire is their second element), or dark pants with light-colored barely visible striped dress-shirts. Everything that creates a high contrast makes metal people feel even more disciplined than they already are which invigorates and pleases them. Metals may wear contrasting clothes all the time without giving much thought to why they feel comfortable in this particular type of dress. But if they give it a thought they might soften their appearance by choosing softer colors or by avoiding obvious symmetry in their clothing. This slight change may help them in their communication with other elements, especially trees and fires. It may also help metals feel more relaxed.

I cannot help but mention that the type of dress code naturally preferred by the metals has become the "uniform" for work at the office or in job interviews. Because when it comes to being perceived as a hardworking, socially reliable person, our society trusts metal people like no one else!

Metal people are advised to become fully aware that they are innately drawn to contrasting and symmetrical patterns, so they can utilize them mindfully as energy-boosters. Metal energy does need balancing using other elements, such as fire, tree, or earth energy. However, the first step towards an individual's balance begins by embracing one's own element fully. By loving yourself just as God created, not as others desire you to be. With this in mind, I highly recommend metals regularly practice mindful use of symmetrical and/or contrasting patterns. One such practice of my metal friends is to draw the "Flower of Life" or other sacred geometry patterns. It boosts their energy and desire to work for other's wellbeing, all the while reminding them that the ultimate symmetry and order are in the hands of the Divine Creator and therefore their personal motivations for working hard must be pure.

When it comes to food preference, metal people have a natural taste for sour and pickled. You can bet someone is a metal if they eat plenty of pickled cucumbers, olives, sauerkraut, or enjoy vinegar, mustard, and other similar things. In fact, because of their internally contrasting and contradictory nature, metal people cannot stand bland foods. They always need a counterpoint for everything, including food. Eggs are never eaten alone. They will likely need plenty of ketchup or sprouted grain toast to go with it. They will often eat every single bite of their eggs with toast in their mouth simultaneously! Metals love contrast in terms of food, but it has to be juxtaposed – neutral plus flavorful.

Autumn is the metal person's time of year. Understandably, metals enjoy the plethora of contrast present in changing autumn leaves. The season provides a refreshing juxtaposition with early morning cold weather, warmer temperatures during daylight hours, and freezing temperatures at night. Autumn days also bring the endless stretch of summer heat to an end, which has a tendency to melt down the metal people's will-power.

This leads us to conclude that metals who are severely out of shape, need take a vacation, while those metals who feel strong and are in good shape should tackle particularly daunting tasks during the months of autumn. Either way, things run much smoother for the metals, (people show less resistance to their will) if they move ahead with their plans during the September-October season.

Late afternoon provides metals with an abundance of their own element. Naturally, when business is all taken care of, and the "to-do" list is complete, metals can begin to unwind according to their own perfect relaxation plan. Metal people love afternoons, but love them organized. A concert date scheduled a month in advance, an evening dedicated to cleaning out the attic, or a perfect dinner party for a select group of people is ideal for what a metal person considers an evening well spent. Never forget metal people are the most dedicated and organized gym users, exercisers, joggers, and Qigong practitioners. They allocate time in the later part of the afternoon for self-improvement, whether it is a fitness program, language lessons, or neighborhood projects. In other words, how metals spend their evenings looks like work to the tree and fire people. However, this is perfect for the metals and should be explained to their partners and family, because they do worry about them. They measure their lack of time spent doing nothing by their own experience of enjoying such activities, believing that metal-people never stop to enjoy themselves, but they do. Just in a different way. Not by being lazy like an Earth person, or watching an emotional movie, like a tree person. This *is not* relaxation for a metal person, as it actually strains their Qi resources. They often participate in "meaningless" activities against their wishes to "do right" by their partners. So, stop forcing them to relax according to your own model,

Metals are happiest after all their work is done at sunset

because what metals hate most are idleness, uselessness, and overflowing emotional engagements with others. After work they like to be active, focused on goal accomplishments, including the noble goal of saving the planet and its inhabitants. As for parties, (especially for metals grown out of college age) they are not particularly tempting to attend. They truly only enjoy parties and recreational events that follow their own agendas. For this reason, it is either sporting events or small gatherings at their own house where they know who will do what and what they can do about it.

In terms of cardinal directions, metals are traditionally associated with the West. Western civilization is very metallic in nature and people with an abundance of metal generally fare better in Western countries than they do in Africa or Asia. Metals who wish to boost their energies may benefit from moving to New Mexico, Utah, Arizona or western Texas. When building a residence, the western areas of the city or town are the most ideal, where the sunset governs the landscape. Getting lots of access to western light through windows, porches or bench located by or directly on the western wall provides significant power-boosting to the metals.

One peculiar observation is due; California and Hawaii (because of proximity to Asia) do not embrace the energy of the West, and instead are in harmony with the East. This is why people born with the tree energy feel so welcome and become empowered when they move to these two states.

The organ-system metal people rely on most for their natural power are; lungs, bronchia, and the respiratory tract. Because metal people like to be in charge of everything, they usually talk for long hours. They don't think surroundings are very important, so they scream their commands outdoors in any kind of weather (rain or snow) or lock themselves indefinitely in dusty, poorly ventilated offices without stepping outside for fresh air. This is why by the end of most days, metal people experience sore throats, but pay no attention. Metals are also poor breathers. Most of the time they act under stress, their muscles tense, and breath shallow. As a result, metal people are often sick with flus and colds.

By taking good care of their respiratory organs, it is possible for metals to retain high levels of energy throughout their life. Although metals prefer sophisticated exercises in a gym, simple exercises executed at home or the office work much better for them. One such exercise is singing. A metal person should go on a little walk while humming or quietly singing a simple tune. If a metal person has a good voice they can sing in a choir or take private singing lessons. An important thing to remember here is to sing without competing. Sing so happiness rises from the lungs and middle and lower sections of the body. Also effective for boosting lung-power, are relaxed swimming and dancing. Once again, these must be practiced for pleasure, not competition. Finally, Qigong breathing like Nine-breath Method, Yoga and meditation are extremely good for the metals, but many of them find it difficult to stop thinking and concentrate only on their breath.

Chapter Twelve

Energy Boosters for the Earth People

Unlike other elements, Earth people rarely become utterly exhausted or depleted of Qi. This is exactly why the power of this element is so greatly valued throughout all Asian societies. In Tibet, China, Vietnam and Japan, political leaders were always sought among people whose innate Qi was the Earth element. When one has Earth element, it makes cultivating and mastering all other elements much easier. People who carry Earth Qi in their biomagnetic field are good for people with the other four elements, as they help them connect with each other and understand and appreciate their differences.

In terms of beneficial colors, Earth people may look no further than the color of Earth itself. Indeed, everything brownish, brownish-greenish, brownish-blackish and brownish-purplish remind us of the surface of the Earth serving as a powerful energy-booster for the Earth people. Most of them are aware of this. One of my Earth-friends makes her own power-days by wearing the American military uniform. The uniform is designed as camouflage and to be indistinguishable from the ground where a soldier drops for cover. Another Earth person I know feels his best days are when he wears his special "Quicksilver" t-shirt, which is purplish-brownish in color – "a little bit like the painted desert" -- while the quicksilver logo reminds him of rich minerals hidden inside the Earth.

Some Earth people are naturally drawn to yellow colors and gold. Their Qi is increased by wearing gold jewelry and clothes in gold and yellow colors.

When the Earth people choose their power-colors to wear, they must also remember their sensitivity to the feel of fabric against their skin. Wearing only 100% natural fabric provides their bodies with pleasant tactile sensation every time they feel the fabric across the body. This is guaranteed to help the Earths make it through the day with significantly less stress compared to days when they wear a metal person's "uniform" -- white top and dark bottom. Additional word of advice -- Earths should avoid wearing "all black." They look sexy when they do, but this should be reserved for the rare occasion to impress someone taking the Earth's physical attractiveness for granted.

In terms of culinary tastes, Earth gains energy from a variety of tastes, none of which should be over-consumed; fires benefit by eating spicy and hot temperature foods, but Earths must eat less than fires and keep them less spicy. Metals depend on sour and vinegary tastes for maintaining high levels of energy. Earths need a dose of sour in the diet as well, but once again, for dishes to be beneficial they must be less sour and vinegary and they should consume less of them. The same rule applies to bitter and sweet foods. In short, the best diet for the Earth can be called bland or neutral, where everything is kept in-check.

When the Earth person is in distress (which is rarely) a trip to a nearby restaurant and ordering a Thanksgiving dinner can be just the right medicine. If an Earth-person has a strong second element they will benefit by eating foods associated with the power of that second element – hot and spicy for the secondary fire, pickles and mustard for the secondary metal, chocolate for the secondary tree, and adding some salt to food for the secondary water.

The season most supportive of the Earth element's power is the so-called Indian summer. Earths feel more active, and do much better socially, right when the summer is about to end and turn into fall. Earths also do very well during all transitional periods, such as between winter and spring. Their strongest time is not during the winter, as it is for the waters, but when the snow is about to thaw, producing the first signs of spring. At the same time, Earth does not always feel strong during the high point of spring. Tree-people feel really empowered then, but Earths resist the temptation to be naturally inspired and swept off their feet by omnipresent romantic feelings.

If you are an Earth person you might know what I am talking in what follows. Not during the seasons, rather *in between seasons*, other people feel out of touch with their elements, while Earth-people actually become strong and feel quite at home. If it is not "springy" enough for the tree-people it is just perfect for the Earths. If it's not summery enough for the fires, it'll be perfect for the Earths! And so on. Earths should start noticing the days when things are in flux, not one way or the other. On these days, their innate Earth element is going to be the strongest. During these in between-season days, people with other elements will be much more responsive to the needs of the Earth people and more attentive to their messages.

For their own comfort Earths enjoy; lukewarm temperatures, a slight breeze with some clouds and nothing extreme. So, on the days when the world is like that, feel your vibrations enhanced, feel God's will more opened toward you and make those important decisions, which, I know you do not like to make, unless your second element is fire or metal. If there is no need to make a decision, just turn such days into a pleasure-gathering. Go out and enjoy nature, get together with friends to play music or nice games. When the weather is *neutral*, it is the time when the Earth person needs to make a call to a boy-friend, or girl-friend, and finally tell them the truth. It is the time to contact their out-of-state or out of the country family members, or move to another house. (I know you dislike even the thought of moving, this is why I say it!)

The best time for the Earths is early afternoon. A reminder; Waters must have their night hours in order to be themselves and feel as happy as can be. Fires can claim their high hour any time of day or night, but it's around noon, when the Sun is high, they are at their strongest. Trees must utilize their morning hours to benefit themselves and strengthen their nerves for the day ahead. Metals can relax when they schedule their time off during the late afternoon. And Earths must recharge their batteries daily during the early afternoon.

My younger son is an Earth person, and I observed for years how he intuitively followed his own bio-magnetic rhythms, which are very different from mine or that of my husband, his father. After he returned from school around two p.m. he did nothing of importance. Although he had tons of homework, or friends would call him, inviting to go out for sports or fun, he ignored it all. Instead, he spent a couple of hours hanging out, playing with his cat, eating snacks, reading a little bit of this, a little bit of that, listening to his music, and then he would go on a walk or take a short nap. Around five p.m. his energy shifted dramatically and he would be fully recharged, ready to go out with friends, or begin seriously studying. This schedule is ideal for the Earth person if they can arrange it. The early afternoons should be "sacred" for the Earths, because this particular stretch of time can give them the biggest boost in their energy-levels.

The cardinal direction of the Earth element is center. I hope you still remember that the tree element does better under the influence of eastern directions (which in the USA is also found in California and Hawaii due to their proximity to Asia). Metals do best under the influence of Western

Daydreaming is one way the Earth person recharges

directions, while north, north-east, and north-west are the best locations for the water element. Earths may discover they have more energy and their lives are easier residing in locations toward the center of a country, such as the American mid-west. Iowa, Indiana or even South or North Dakota would be ideal places for the Earth person. They may feel more at home in these state's local culture and natural environments, and perhaps they will exert less effort in order to succeed socially, economically and personally.

Earths are the balance-keepers. Because of this, they lack a desire to travel even for the sake of finding romantic love and sexual engagement. Naturally, there is even less desire to travel for work and business. Earths must arrange their lives to travel short distances between their various focal points. In other words, for the Earths it is always better to be situated close to a central point where all their activities intersect. This means Earths may not do very well in a big city like New York or Los Angeles unless they can arrange their lives allowing them to mainly stay in one particular neighborhood where everything is interconnected. Similarly, Earths might not do well in densely forested places where movements are obstructed by natural conditions and requires lots of personal effort to get somewhere. If it requires *too much effort* to get somewhere due to natural obstacles and limitations, the Earths will sit in one place, and this may not be such good thing. Areas with too many mountains, which are difficult to traverse, or areas that require much travel by water are not ideal for the Earths either, although some access to a body of water is usually positive.

The internal organ most supportive of the earth element is stomach. Some Chinese doctors call it – spleen – others both spleen and stomach. All activities which affect proper functioning of the stomach (and spleen) also activate and enhance the flow of Qi in people with the Earth element.

Thus, if you are an earth element, joyful eating must be recognized as vital and never be sacrificed for anything else. But because food is so good for the Earths they may have a tendency toward accumulating extra-weight. This is why activities and exercises designed to move energy around the mid-section of the body are the best for the Earths. These include tennis, ping-pong, hula-hooping, swimming, gentle yoga, breathing exercises and Qigong that emphasizes being rooted into the ground. While engaging in these activities one must remember Earths are not competitive. Competition runs against their nature, and if they get involved in recreational activities which lead to self-deprecation, heated debates, or hurt feelings, such exercises do no good.

Drinking tea regularly is another great habit recommended to all the Earth people, especially if these teas are designed to increase the health of the stomach, such as chamomile, peppermint or a mild ginger.

Part Three

5-Elements in Romantic Relationships

As thought it was yesterday, I clearly remember what my Daoist teacher taught me about romantic relationships. In reality it was many decades ago and since those days studying with him I've received thousands of confirmations of his accuracy on this subject. I did not have any romantic relationships of my own during the years I studied with him, but I did experience plenty of opportunities to observe how others struggled and suffered in relationships with those whom they seemed to love most. I was seventeen, three years away from loosing my virginity and receiving the Soviet Union style of initiation into womanhood.

My teacher said to me; "Energy that runs through people's relationships is one of the strongest energies on Earth, especially if it involves sexual intimacy. Think about it, Tanya, most of the things we see, touch and move with our hands are not allowed to penetrate our physical bodies. Only air, food, drink and our love-partner receive our permission to go deep, very deep inside our skin. Thus, the energy exchange that happens through romantic, intimate loving can either make you strong and healthy, or it can weaken and destroy you. People seldom realize this when they initiate a merging of Qi and Jing by uniting with each other through physical love. They generate such a high level of new energy that one can make an atomic bomb from it, or use it for electricity...enough to light up a whole city in Siberia." He laughed then, his eyes mischievous yet sincere. "Out of this energy of merging of the female and male Qi and Jing a whole new human being can be created. You just think about this -- No amount of human effort put together for many years in many different laboratories around the world can create one little baby, but a couple of lovers can do it in one hour or less! Is this truly a powerful energy or what! This is why lovers who do not wish to create a baby just yet, can use this energy to heal each other, to make each other smarter and more courageous. Through this powerfully intimate, love-unity humans can heal their environment and take care of each political problem they have. In your Western societies' literature, love always disobeys the old rules instilled by families, religions or race and national discriminations. Love is the power behind the most magnificent breaking of old boundaries that used to separate all of humanity. Love, especially romantic love is the engine for miracle making. But just like atomic energy it can be used toward a horrible end if personal hunger for power becomes the driving force for its use. Humans may destroy themselves by frivolously and dangerously using their new sexual power without proper knowledge of how it works. And this is why my life in China has been spared, Tanya, so that I can talk to you and others who will become teachers one day."

My Daoist teacher mastered the art of sexual healing. Several of his female students had sexual relations with him as part of their training, although I did not. Some were healed of various heath problems and attained radiant Qi as a result of their mutual energy exchange. Sex certainly has great healing power when used by people who truly understand it. During my training with him I remained celibate and therefore I often could not understand (due to lack of life experience) why friends and classmates I knew were able to hate so strongly someone they said they loved.

Being instructed by my teacher later helped me through several challenging relationships without loosing my original supply of Qi and Jing. Preserving one's energy in an intimate relationship and increasing it with the help of your partner, to be empowered and healed as well, is the main goal behind teaching 5-Elements for personal relationships.

The following descriptions are radically different from what one usually finds in various horoscopes or self-help books. The main difference is about gaining and loosing Qi and physical vitality through relationships, which can result in powerful healing or serious depression, even disease. The illustration to what will be covered in this conversation can be found in the world of nature. If you plant a cactus in a swamp, there is very little chance that it will survive. And if you plant a Siberian cypress in a Mohave Desert it will surely die unless every day of your life you provide that tree with artificial watering and protection from sun. Meaning, certain peoples' energy-fields are so incompatible in terms of their 5-element structure that, simply by sharing living space, they may be able to destroy each others vital energies, causing regular irritations and annoyance and eventually creating such a significant loss of vitality that it may take years to restore it.

I am not saying that we are exactly like those plants. God created us differently from them and yet, God made us a part of this natural world. If the Creator wanted us to exist entirely separate and independently from all laws of nature, a separate environment would most certainly have been made for us. But instead, the holy scriptures are full of images of trees, flowers and bushes, as well as images of water and fire, and also swords, shields and chariots made of metal, which conveys an important message for us -- We are expected to live in harmony with the nature that has been created for us, both on the inside and outside of us.

As I describe relationships between the 5-elements that are particularly difficult to master, I don't want you to think it is all-negative and that these combinations can never work out. But I do want you to realize how challenging it is when the opposing elements, such as water and fire, or tree and metal, fall in love with each other, and begin sharing their lives and their energies *everyday*. It is difficult, and you will need all the help you can get. This certainly involves calling on God's powers and praying for help. But it is also extremely helpful to fully understand how your partner's element is different from yours.

Chapter Thirteen

Love Between the Fire and Water

In this chapter, we are going to talk about the most challenging and energy-draining 5-elements combination in personal relationships. But we will also talk about how through strong faith, prayer and knowledge – we can use these challenges for spiritual growth and wisdom which, in the end, are the most precious possessions we humans can ever obtain while being here on Earth. If we approach these most challenging 5-elements relationships without a prayer to the Divine Power, or the knowledge necessary for personal transformation, we will most likely suffer from serious depletion of personal Qi, as well as inflict grievous damages to our partners, simply because we are unaware of the daily mechanics of the transference of Qi taking place between the partners.

Let us begin by looking at what happens when fire and water fall in love with each other. This is considered a classic type of romance, commonly known through the expression, "opposites attract." Sung through countless songs and portrayed in hundreds of novels and movies, everyone is at least superficially familiar with this type of love. But do we understand what is really happening when the fire and water begin to work their love relationship between each other? Let us take a closer look.

In the older days, when women were not allowed to socially express their innate fire, this archetype of love involved a fiery, risk-taking, ultimately self-assured, male who would fall in love with a mysterious woman with a "dark past" or "seductive inclinations," capable of keeping her "deadly secrets" until it was too late for the male to recognize the danger and extricate himself from the situation. Such stories inevitably end in disaster of some sort for the fire-male. Unable to truly "possess" his mysterious, ever-changing, mermaid-like lover, he gives himself to gambling, drinking, various crimes and other socially unacceptable behavior, because this is his only way to fully participate and finally draw in the waters of her ultimately, unconquerable sexual beauty.

In recent decades, I saw an amazing shift in the way the fire-water couple gets organized. I cannot account for all of the U.S.A., but at least in my home state of California, I see more fire-females drawn to the water-males than the other way around. *The fire-person of either gender is attracted to the water-person, because fire is turned on by the challenge and ultimately the impossibility, as fire cannot burn water.* Often fire goes quickly through her or his relationships, because their victories come soon and they quickly "devour" all that was there in another person. Then they become bored and need a new challenge, which is why they unconsciously feel pushed to begin new relationships on a regular basis. However, this model does not work for the water-partner.

The fire-person finds a worthy opponent in the quiet, withdrawn lover who never asks for much, never fights back, is always present and yet, can never be conquered no matter how hot the fire's temperament might become. In the end, the fire-person may find herself (himself) "stuck" in a relationship with the water person, eventually falling either head-over-heels in love or in sort of a sickening manner of being in love with the water-partner.

The fire-lover may be "stuck" with the water partner as a result of all other elements rejecting him or her. See, the fire-person loves with such intensity, speed and passion that it makes all other elements, including tree, water, earth and metal, grow weary of them and no longer wish to withstand the unpredictable flame moving across the fabric of their lives, nor do they wish or have the health condition allowing them to be subjected to the fire's brutal and all-consuming style of relationship. So, let me explain what happens, energetically, as the fire-lover engages people with four other elements and why fire may be forced to finally settle in a relationship with a water-partner or remain alone through the rest of her or his days.

Fire is naturally drawn to people with tree energy. Fires are much more naturally drawn to them than they are drawn to the water-people. However, fire goes through the love of a tree person very quickly, burning most of what the tree has to offer. Sweet sentimentality of a tree-personality, refreshing in the beginning, eventually, leads to boredom and irritation. No longer is this behavior appreciated by a fierce fighter, which every fire-person carries within. Tired of always protecting the weaker partner, fire begins to see this sweetness as nothing more than foolishness – How can a person act nicely to all people, all the time and defend one's own interests? At this point in the relationship, the fire-lover loses appreciation of the tree's character and goes into regular outbursts of anger against the tree's weakness and their inability to protect themselves. The tree-lover may need to work up enough courage to terminate the relationship. If the tree-person does not do so in time, with enough life-force preserved to begin a restoration, the resulting tree-personality may be a completely devastated human being with a tendency towards permanent depression or various maniacal disorders.

When fire falls in love with fire, they too will be very close to destroying each other. Sure, this will be one of the most unforgettable relationships for both of them, but unless one of the fire partners has a strong secondary element, the relationship may lead to the most brutal fights one has ever seen. These fights will surely draw into the flames many innocent by-standers, such as the two lovers' friends, relatives and neighbors. When the two fires fight for supremacy, they are capable of the wildest steps including physical injury to each other and their properties. Even serious attempts at each other's lives are possible, for the passion burns so hot. This, of course, cannot last for long. Like putting out a forest-fire by setting another fire, these two will burn each other out. Or because the fire-lover always seeks to expand and "set on fire some new burnable lovers," the two will not burn each other, but be distracted by other partners.

Earth can make a good lover for the fire, but only if and when the fire is ready to slow down and lead a more stable life. Otherwise, this kind of relationship will be a bore to the fire. There is not much challenge in this romance for the fire unless the Earth-personality has tree or metal as their secondary elements, which can add exciting sparks to this relationship.

Metal has very good potential for a healthy relationship with the fire-personality, and we will cover this later in our book. Here, we will simply note that with the metal-person, the fire's behavior is not as harmful, for metal can withstand the fire's heat, but it can also limit the fire's ability to burn. So the fire who is young and looking for an adventurous romance will feel limited and disempowered by the metal. Using a smart analogy here, a young person who wishes to be a wild forest fire or a volcano is going to feel like a camp-fire limited by the metal lining inside the fire-pit.

Against the dynamics of the aforementioned relationships, the fire's relationship with the water appears to be most challenging, most exciting and able to last. The fire-lover gets to burn that which is unburnable, hence the excitement and challenge attracts them. Because waters are usually quiet partners, it gives fire the deepest satisfaction of being able to say crazy things and do crazy stuff all the time without being punished or without feeling guilty for ruining someone's life. The fire person operates under the illusion they will never run out of fuel or material to burn. At the same time, water moves easily in response to the fire's hot temperatures, thus creating another illusion of being affected by the fire, yet never truly hurt. If the fire becomes too much, water evaporates, but then it condenses into itself again. So, the fire can enjoy the partner and stay around this person longer than they can with anyone else.

Water reflects the fire's brilliance like no other partner. The fire person is usually narcissistic and self-absorbed, but the water-person does not mind because they are absorbed in her/his own way. The illusion once again is of the fire-person being totally accepted and understood, yet the water could not care less for her lover's fiery ways of being. This analysis may convince us water is fire's best choice for a lover, however, it is not so. Actually, other elements are more ideally suited for the fire as lovers if only fire could stand character cultivation and impose self-restrictions for the sake of other people. This is because water only creates the illusion of satisfaction and of being engaging with the fire. While fire runs its unpredictable course and uses tons of energy to sustain the relationship, the water-partner usually remains psychologically withdrawn and mentally cold, minding his own business all the time. Yet fire, who pays little attention to subtle clues of other people's behavior, knows nothing about the "real life" of the water person all the while drawing deeper and deeper into their energy-field capable of total destruction of its vitality.

For fires the challenge of boiling a water partner is alluring

Specifically, in a romantic relationship that involves intimacy, where the Qi and Jing are exchanged at the deepest level of the body, mind and soul, as the fire-person moves deeper and deeper into the water energy, he or she loses more and more physical warmth, becoming strangely calmer and colder. The damage to the life force of the fire becomes significant fairly early in the relationship and yet, this loss of personal power is usually experienced by the fire as deep peace following sexual intercourse. In reality, it is a severe depletion of the fire's energy that they previously had not known in their other relationships (where their partners felt the depletion). This situation needs to be understood and discussed between the love partners or it can lead to serious physical and mental problems.

The fire is not just being satisfied or pacified through sex with the water-partner, but is actually losing vital force. This is experienced in a very familiar form of feeling more passive and having diminished capabilities on all fronts the day after sexual union took place. Sometimes, several days after making love with the water-lover, the fire-person feels weak and yet somehow feels good about continuing the relationship. The kidneys-world, which is ruled by water and roughly corresponds to the entire lower abdomen of human body both outside and inside, is usually bearing the brunt of this challenging relationship. Fire lovers who are regularly sleeping with the water-partners may experience pain or various problems with the low back (usually, in the sciatica area, but if the relationship is old, it can be even higher on the spine), or problems with the urinal and genital systems. In terms of visible changes in one's behavior, the fire-person involved in making love to a water-person may lose the ability to create freely and abundantly and is no longer engaged in spontaneous, multiple projects. The fire can lose boldness and the ability to quickly jump from one thing to another, to travel to distant places on a short note, and is filled with doubt and self-deprecation.

In this particular fire to water romantic relationship, fire usually sustains more damage than the water does. Since fire-people are unfamiliar with the concept of impossibility, they will not accept 'no' for an answer. Fires will keep trying and burning. HOPING that the water will turn into oil and fire, at last, will have the desirable explosion of passion. They are sure that one day their water-companion will go as crazy for them as they are for their dark and mysterious ocean-like nature, but that day may never come.

Although the damage to the water is less than to the fire, there is still some loss. The major disservice is how fire enhances the water's main emotion -- fear. Because fire is so restless and unpredictable, water can never rely on its fiery partner. Water already has difficulty making sense of its own existence, so additional restlessness and unnecessary danger from the fire's life-style, are not healthy for the water. Water may be pushed into further isolation, desiring to be alone, locked in a room with alcohol or on the computer for many hours in a row. Yet, it will be fire's health problems that are most difficult to fix.

Despite these cautions, please keep in mind that with higher cultivation and faith in God's miraculous powers, all types of relationships can become possible. Just be aware of these energies in a relationship. Realize that you and your beloved, like all life forms, exist inside a specific biomagnetic field of energy, which we activate every time we engage with someone by merely being alive. If you maintain this awareness, all the pairings can be mutually beneficial, however some of them require more effort and a higher degree of cultivation, just like the water-fire relationships.

Chapter Fourteen

Love Between the Metal and Tree

You may notice sometimes as you talk to someone (not necessarily your lover) for fifteen minutes or less, you walk away from them feeling angry, anxious or deeply unhappy. But why did this happen? Why did such a short exchange of energy lead to unpleasant results? Often times, the explanation cannot be found from one's actions or words, because in fact it's due to your and the other person's elemental energies interacting. In these cases, the elemental energies from both parties are set to self-destruct mode from the beginnings of time. Yes, from the beginnings of time, just as a large body of water can extinguish fire, and a large ax can cut down a tree.

Let me give you an example; you are a tree person and the person you recently spoke to is ruled by metal. Metal does not value emotions and feels uncomfortable when others display them. Metals value clearly defined goals and specific plans leading to an accomplishment. You pay a visit to your metal friend or boss to share information you collected through your emotional life. For instance, you share a concern about the wellbeing of another co-worker, or your boss' son or your friend's wife. Ultimately as a tree-person, this is what you care about; feeling how other people go about their lives and sharing this emotional information in an attempt to help through love and compassion, or at least by commiserating with another's suffering. This is how the tree energy survives and orients itself in life. And is directly opposite to how the metal energy survives and *makes itself useful*.

The metal person's response to your concerns may include one of the following: 1) this is none of my business, let these people sort out their own problems; 2) what are you proposing? If you aren't proposing anything, there is nothing to talk about; 3) let us talk about it another time, I am too busy now (meaning, I never want to talk about this again). Energetically speaking, this metal person has chop-chop-chop, chopped some of your most precious branches, making you feel unwanted, unappreciated and possibly even stupid for wanting to talk about such things.

Therefore as a general rule, for couples intimately sharing their lives with each other, the structure of the metal person is often experienced as very cutting and hurtful to a tree person, *no matter* how or what they are talking about, or what sorts of problems or business they are dealing with. The metal person finds it to be very useful to shape a tree person according to designs of his or her own, similar to trees and bushes in public spaces. But as a native tree person, you absolutely cannot find any use for geometrical shapes or the process of cutting. For a tree-person, the most important, internal mission is to grow as many branches as possible; they will grow and sustain an enormous amount of branches without ever asking if these branches are useful. Their branches are useful to them, because they exist and are beautiful and alive. *However, for a metal-person, everything must have a purpose, a reason, a goal.* There must be a perceivable structure and organization to everything they do and for everyone they approach. So, if as a tree person you shared your experience with a metal in a brief, fifteen-minute exchange, you may have lost three branches or more, depending on whether the metal person has perfected him/herself to a chain-saw or remained with a regular ax.

*With good intentions, metals often 'shape' tree partners
into neatly groomed hedges using critical remarks*

Picture this situation repeating itself everyday (and in the case of lovers, every night). Although the tree people are endowed with amazing agility and can re-grow quickly, still they cannot grow branches fast enough to compensate for the work of an ax, especially a chainsaw. The metal partner can be very committed to accomplishing his or her goal and may not stop shaping their tree-lover, according to their specific vision, until they are nearly dead with nothing left for further shaping. Sad, isn't it? It happens all the time though and everyday I see among my many friends and students how the metal and tree continue to torture each other without the slightest idea of what is going on.

I do not mean to say that the tree and metal can never be together in a loving, respectful even fruitful relationship. But I do say this is a monumental task to take on and is much more challenging than building a relationship between the tree and water, or between the earth and metal elements. So, you see my friends, this is not so much a matter of whether you like or dislike someone, or whether you feel you have the right to be in any kind of relationship you choose for yourself. It is a matter of respecting the nature of things as they are, as they have been created. I suggest we approach our relationships with the same seriousness which a good gardener approaches her work. She will not plant firs and ferns on the sun-exposed terrace, or rosebushes in a swamp or wetland. Good lovers must realize that due to their elemental powers, some people will uphold us and our life-force will increase as a result of our loving, while other people, due to the same reason, hold the power to destroy our health and life.

If you carefully read the description of the fire-water romantic story, you probably noticed the water does not go around searching for fire, hoping to conquer it. Instead, water waits for whoever comes their way, and if it happens to be a fire, so be it. Similarly, when an "aggressor" falls in love with his or her "victim," this applies to the love often seen between the metal and tree personalities. The tree person does not ask the metal, "Please, cut me down. I'm tired of my life," rather it is the metal person who comes with an ax intending on making a nice house out of the tree.

This is how it starts; the metal person begins searching for a suitable mate, which for them is always a rational procedure. So, my dear tree and fire people, be aware the metal person falls in love in a much more rational fashion than any of you. A famous online program, called "The GAME," has been created by metal-males. The game gives words and actions that when followed, allow a man to walk away from any party with a girl he wishes to attract. In the United States, metal is identified with strong masculinity, and these metal males idealize their ultimate feminine counterpart as the tree-woman. Think about it; the fire-girl is too crazy or embarrassing. The water-girl too gothic and possibly involved in drugs (metal is not terribly interested in mind-alteration, because the mind is their main source of happiness). Metal-girl is a fighter and difficult to win (remember, metal must win at any cost). Thus, the metal-male views the tree-female as his ideal love object, not only because she is easy to win, but also because she can be molded into following whatever his agenda may be. One big reason for this is, she has more *building material* than any other personality and metals are truly proud of their *building plans*. Even the laziest of the metals is industrious in one sense or another and is greatly inspired by the tree-girl's budding wealth of potential.

183

The second (undeniable) line of attraction the metal develops for the female tree-personality stems from his competiveness. The tree-girl is often extremely beautiful (if she is not overweight), just like a tree or flower in the garden, and she becomes a trophy for the metal-man to win for himself. She is pleasing to his rational thoughts about what love should be, which includes taking care of his biological needs.

The metal man knows in order to satisfy his biological needs, he either needs a series of one-night stands or a constant companion; tree fits the bill. There are movies about the archetypal tree-woman, falling deeply in love with an Earth-man. But she ends up being won over by a metal-man who does not love her as the Earth-guy truly does, but who is capable of winning her over and keeping her as his trophy. This happens in the real world too. Metal may protect his "tree-woman prize" by defending her with a "metal weapon". His weapon is usually money, a fully metallic, archetypal vibration, because up until only recent history most of the world's currency was made out of metal and even now money's value depends on its gold equivalent.

There is yet another line of magnetic attraction the metal has with tree-woman. From his deep loneliness, feeling sorry for himself and his sense of isolation from most people and nature, metal attracts the tree-woman through her compassion for him. But she usually ends up in a metal trap, as her soft energy is unable to fix the ultimate hardness of the metal. How can you fix a metal machine with wooden instruments?

Tree may have difficulty nurturing a strong metal partner

Once the attraction has been established and regular sexual intercourse between the tree and the metal lovers takes place, their bio-magnetic fields begin to act upon each other, always causing wear and tear in one direction. The soft wood is damaged by the harshness of the metal, and there is an overall loss of energy unless the metal cultivates and becomes more like water. When a craftsman cuts a statue out of a wild oak, the oak is not so happy, what do you think? This is a description of how the tree-female can lose her energy to a metal-male. By the way, the reverse is also possible, when the metal-lady picks up the tree-guy for her love carving, but we will address this later.

For a tree-woman, emotions are nurturing, but for a metal person, emotions are destructive. In other words, fluids and dampness are good for the tree, yet rust most metals. The tree-lover must love by constantly generating and exchanging feelings. The metal person primarily loves through actions. The metal person who cares about his love shows it by being on time for a date. This is completely unimportant for the tree person. The tree-woman doesn't care if he is on time or not. What she cares about is the expression on his face and his first words to her. The moment he says, "My dear, you are 15 minutes late!" the first branch of her happiness is cut off, falling with a thump to the ground. But let us read the message recorded in the metal-man's mind, "She is late. She doesn't respect me. If she doesn't respect me she cannot love me." Compare this with the tree-girl's internal dialogue, "I spent all this extra time making myself beautiful for you and I am so full of love for you. How can you not see this? And why does it matter that I am fifteen minutes late?" As she is deeply hurt by his failure to recognize her love and beauty, she closes up, with a sad expression upon her face. Then he asks, "What is wrong?" Because now it is his turn to express his particular form of discontent, "What I said is right. You cannot deny that you were late, therefore I'm right with my remark." No matter how many hours of continued observation of this relationship, her side is consistently hurt by the lack of consideration for her emotions, beauty and expressions of kindness and love, while his side continues being perplexed by the fact that he cannot express what is right, because every time he states the fact, the tree-partner closes up and starts crying. This is clearly a matter of two bio-magnetic fields resonating at different levels. For the tree woman it is all about how *it feels to do certain things or be engaged in certain types of activities.* I'm not saying that the tree-women are not capable of rational thinking, they are, however in matters of love they tend to favor emotional factors. But the metal-male rarely relies on feelings alone. He thinks all the time, aside from the few minutes right before and during his orgasm (true of the metal woman as well). For the metal person it is practically impossible to shake off thinking unless he stubbornly masters the art of meditation, where he does not dissolve into nothingness, like other elements, but commands his mind to stop.

His "secret love affair with his own thoughts" makes him an architect, instead of a tender lover. He plans it all out, "I have to go to work in 15 minutes, and so I should kiss her now." Or, "Because I'm not going to see her again until next week, it should be more than a gentle kiss, it should lead to intimacy." In the end intimacy often takes place as a result of his decision, and the tree-girl often experiences "his precise plan" instead of love. For a metal-man, the time elapsed between his thought, "I want to have sex" and getting ready for it, is short, but for a tree-woman it is not. This is why in many situations she is taken physically without the necessary readiness on her part.

It is unfortunate that this form of sexual behavior became society's archetype for an ideal lover. In most of our movies we see the unstoppable, always ready for sex, love-machine who takes but an instant to get into action. Yet, for the tree-lover, it is all about the right time and the right kind of feelings that make sex pleasurable. However, out of kindness toward her lover, the tree-woman allows him to do what she ultimately does not like, or shows just enough resistance to arouse him, making him think it is fake, a way to attract him. Therefore, physical diseases of the tree female are sometimes related to an emotional sense of violation, being taken without her desires taken into consideration and disrespect. She may develop unexplainable headaches, anxiety symptoms or panic attacks in less than three years from the beginning of the relationship with the metal-male. Also, because during the regular 'rapes' where she is not ready for intercourse, she may forget to breathe and therefore respiratory problems can accumulate. More colds and sore throats are common when the tree-woman is with a metal partner. In some cases, the tree-woman can be reduced to a mere stump, sitting behind closed doors, unable to communicate with the outside world. Yet, she would never blame her metal-husband or lover because of her kind character. Metal men do not necessarily act as violent abusers of women, although some of them do, especially if they perceive themselves as losers in other areas of their lives. But many of them pride themselves as righteous, logical, dutiful men who are good providers, and they cannot understand why their wives continue getting sicker and sicker. The diagnosis here is a deficiency of emotional nurturing, as well as disruption of her natural rhythms. Like a tree forced to bloom out of season, it cannot thrive. A balance must be found for this pair to work out.

The kindhearted tree and willful metal people can WORK IT OUT AND MAKE MAGIC if both can grasp the five elements. Recall that water supports tree and metal supports water. If trees can *stop taking things personally* and be patient for the metal to blossom after a hard days work (rather than complain or go into emotional tirades), then there is hope! If a metal partner also remembers his/her water nature and learns to *just be and allow* tree to simply give a massage or loving touch to soften a metallic exterior, there is hope! It's all a matter of both partners embracing WATER. You see, water feeds the tree with patience and understanding, which the metal may be slow to embody, but that is perhaps God's plan for their union in the first place.

If we had partners who did not force us to grow into higher cultivated beings - what good would this life be? Are we here on Earth to experience 'a vacation' where every interaction is perfect? Or are we here to experience life challenges and grow with each other into the higher spiritual beings that we came down here to become?

To the metal and tree couples of the world… you are the future of humanity! If you two cannot get along, how will the metal nations ever get along with the compassionate tree cultures of indigenous people? Perhaps the emotional sobbing of the tree is here to soften a metal's edges that they've had for several lifetimes. Perhaps the tree partner is supposed to stop worrying about what her partner thinks and stop taking his/her obsession with work personally.

Both metal and tree partners are healed when they embrace the water that nurtures them both. Tree becomes more patient with metal and shows more neutrality with regards to taking things personally. Metal allows the tree partner to open their heart and becomes more humble and less domineering. It can work out, but not without serious cultivation of the water element on both sides.

Chapter Fifteen

A New Phenomenon – The Metal Woman

Unlike any other time in human history (except the matriarchal stage of our evolution), modern women in Western-culture societies are fully permitted to express their innate, metallic character. They are now seriously drawn to imitating men's metallic conquest of everything that moves under the Sun, including sports, science, religion, legislation, and military prowess.

In the past, women could rarely indulge in such behavior. Although we often blame women for their lack of rational conductivity in certain situations, we must remember that in the past all forms of strong-willed and strong-minded behavior were trained out of women under severe punishments. Physical beatings and even death were commonplace, because being rational meant critical thinking, comparing and evaluating, and men did not want to see this from women.

If we carefully observe married or long-term couples interact, we notice the male member of the couple will never tolerate any form of public criticism, even for actions that would deserve it in his own mind. He becomes so extremely defensive and unpleasant to his wife or girl-friend that she feels the wound and probably deals with it for a long time. Being criticized (even for a fair reason) by a woman and doing nothing in return, is perceived by the metallic nature of the male as defeat and humiliation. Be aware that in American society, *all* males are trained to have a good dose of metal in their character, regardless of what their innate element might be.

Many people have tried to inform me this is biological, but it is not. It is behavioral, societal training that has continued for at least two thousand years. It taught women how not to use their metal-Qi, and instead get all their needs met through the power of the tree by, "being nice to your guy". Even though women today are generally allowed to possess more metal in their personalities, they still get more from their relationships with men by using their flowery, charming tree-personality than by using their metallic analysis characteristic in the males' behavior. For instance, if she says, "Honey, would you please go to the store and get me some organic coconut-formula milk?" while smiling with her best smile and looking at him with love she is more likely to get what she needs. But if she goes "logical" on him with in a dry, matter-of-fact voice, "My husband, during this last month I marked my calendar and I am saying to you that for 28 days I went to buy the baby formula for our son, but you went only once, and this is why I think today you should go and get the milk," most likely her husband will feel hurt, deeply offended and site a hundred reasons why he shouldn't be going to buy baby's food anyway. *This is why a female metal gets to display her will and logic only if she is in a higher position than a male.* For instance the celebrity-wife or executive-wife who makes more money, has a higher level of education, owns a house or other property and he does not. Even in such cases, one can observe how metal-vibrations built into our males through the social-cultural upbringing begin to go into swing if she goes too far. It's okay for a guy to say, "it's time to go home" and expect she will follow him, but if she says it and adds no explanation such as, "I am not feeling well honey," or better yet, "I have a special surprise for you at home," he would not go right away. He might say, "Stop being so bossy!" or ignore her statement, staying as long as he thinks is necessary. I observed this many times myself. This still strikes me as such an unfair distribution of the permission to use one's will in an open manner.

Today, especially due to the power of money, as we already know money vibrates as quintessential metal-Qi, women get more of their metal rights and this includes increased permission for her to be bossy, and be leader-like not only in the work-place, but also at home and in love relationships. This new metal-woman is a relatively new phenomenon and fun to watch, if of course you do not happen to be one of her lovers. ☺

Metallic-woman is still very much a woman in her body. Her biological form and hormones gives her some Yin energy, therefore she is not totally metallic and machine-like as male metals can be. She retains some flowery grace and elegance of the feminine form and yet, she can use them with such deadly precision that an unprepared man can be incapacitated rather easily. It appears the development of most recent female fashion favors a metallic image of high definition, while our infatuation with the high definition by itself is a part of our enchantment with the female energy gone metallic. Nowadays, the sexually appealing female is the epitomized portrait of a Warrior-Goddess. She walks like a conqueror. She wears her sex like a weapon. She has plenty of sharp lines and straight angles in her clothing and make up. She has developed muscles and is expected to know how to use them, albeit playfully and just to make him feel good about himself!

If you pick up a Sports Illustrated or Cosmo, you'll see the figures of all the female models are flat and sharp everywhere except the breasts. But upon closer inspection of the breasts you may note they are modeled more after the breast-plates of the female warriors in illustrated mythology or comics-books rather than after any woman's real breasts.

This is a message from a metal woman who is now in charge of her own fashion magazines and able to make money on her own beauty. This trend is also forcing men to fall in love with a robot while letting real women have more time for what they really like to do with their lives. In other words, the shapes of the female bodies that used to be portrayed as soft, gentle and relaxed, have now in the high fashion CEO's imagination become swords and shields, complete with the ability to kill him with her beauty, rather than to let him love. It seems that the Mother-Father God has a sense of humor and this reversal is some kind of revenge for the long years of patriarchy women have endured. So, let us now look at specific dynamics of the female metals in love relationships.

Chapter Sixteen

Metal Woman in Romantic Relationships

Very much like her male-metal counterpart, the metal woman is in the relationship for a specific reason. She is not there because of an uncertain emotional need. For her it is often like a game or an interesting battle. She knows what she can get and she enjoys getting it. In otherwords, she may unknowingly act like a huntress whom we used to call Artemis during the high days of Greek civilization. She can be both cold and hot like Artemis. Cold, because Artemis would never be involved on an emotional level with the energies of the creature she hunts. Hot, because Artemis gets feverish and excited by the difficulty, even impossibility of her chase; the more difficult it is to get him to sleep with her the more exciting it is. Did you ever wonder why most powerful women, have had love experiences with men at least a decade younger than them? The answer is simple; because it is challenging enough. This kind of relationship puts her on her tippy toes every day and gives her a huge victory at the same time. The metal-woman knows there are thousands of women younger than her, and she also knows that typically women are younger than their husbands, not the other way around. She says to this, "Look at what I am doing! I am fifty, he is thirty. He is more dedicated to me and more dependent on me than I will ever be! And also, if he looses it and goes away, I can always find another lover but he, cannot." Through this kind of relationship, she receives happiness from getting that which is difficult to obtain. When a fifty year old, financially powerful metal woman finds a man lower in position than herself, but younger in years, to become her lover, this warms her heart.

It pleases her very much and all the while his particular male qualities are not even that important. She does this because she can, she has the power. Metal-women sometimes get their fullest, highest satisfaction from playing with power, just like men used to when we lived in the age of strict patriarchy. Except when the woman does it she is called a bitch and when a man does it he is called a strong character.

However the steady, unwavering rise of the metal woman is a new trend here to stay. This trend is one of the reasons why we see so many (and we are definitely going to see many more) men changing to the female gender, but not the other way around. Just about all transgender men that I know changed their gender for the sake of getting the power they were denied in their masculine shape. All of them had relationships with strong women who refused to surrender and demanded respect for their dignity. Now these transgendered females are doing the same – demanding respect and dignity, but it is hard to get.

For hundreds of years women were not allowed to have any male-like power. Their only power was through seduction and sweet talk. For generations men enjoyed hunting women as if it was a game. Now a new army of the metal women is spreading across the globe and the warrior goddess wants to explore her power. For this reason, she will have no regrets for any of her sexual experiences as she is able to take care of all sorts of possible negative consequences. Her love affairs can sometimes seem like a perfectly executed military campaign or yes, hunting expedition. If her targeted guy is some type of a trophy, that's even better. To be active in initiating the relationship and actually forcing the guy into "doing it," can be biologically satisfying. This is why I do not agree with those who claim submissiveness is a female biological trait. I have observed too many young and mature females to understand that she can enjoy the power game as well as the reward of "getting him" just as much as a man does. A word of warning must be issued here for the metal woman herself and her many lovers. As this warrior is in the habit of taking lovers who are too young, inexperienced, or too competitive, or she simply takes too many lovers, she in fact puts herself in danger of severely destroying her procreative system. Yet, the psychological satisfaction is so great that she may not even realize what is happening. For this reason the greatest danger for the metal woman is to remain childless or lose her ability to conceive. This condition is a direct result of using her sexuality as a weapon. She may also manifest this in STD's.

We talked about the dangers of health that the metal woman exposes herself to in order to celebrate her new social power, but the dangers to her partners are just as great. People endowed with the tree or water or tree-water energy usually become lovers of the metal-woman. This is also true in lesbian relationships where one female is endowed with the metal energy and the other with more of the tree, or water energy. Although as I said, the female biological form softens the workings of the metallic cutting, often injuring character, it is still fully present throughout the relationship. For example, a metal woman routinely disregards her partner's emotions, thinking all conversations about how they feel are expressions of their "weak, sissy or indecisive character." Prone to crying, over-emotional people don't last long in the company of a metal-like female partner. The tree and water partners of the metal-female hear a lot of, "Come on, you! You can do it!" Or, "Grow up already!" Or, "Why can't you be stronger?" And finally, "Don't be such a baby!" Just like the male metal, female metal often refuses to deal with her own emotions or those of her partner. If she begins to feel emotional she often refuses to acknowledge it, because her emotional aspects threaten to weaken her and she cannot stand being weak, so she suppresses them. The female metal may also dislike people who have the capacity to provoke her emotional world, making her reveal the hurt feelings she carries within. She can cut the blooming relationship off immediately if this happens, not bothering to explain to her lover why she cut him or her off so quickly and brutally. It is precisely this kind of behavior that damages her tree-lover.

The tree person who lives his life next to the metal female understands her deep seeded need and tries to teach her what "real" happiness (from the tree-perspective) in a relationship is about. That it cannot be about the conquest all the time, it cannot be about being right all the time, and it is not about being strong all the time. It is about being open toward each other. But in the end, the tree-lover may have to deal with severe injuries, which the metal woman invites upon herself. This can become a life-long problem for the male tree-lover. If she does not cut off her tree-partner's branches, turning him into a bare stump of a man, the tree-lover may eventually have to take complete care of his CEO metal-wife for the rest of their lives, because she simply depleted her life-force through work and competition, thereby remaining in physical decline for her entire latter half of life. By taking care of the two of them the tree-man may deplete his own energy, and become bitter, sour and cynical or all of the above. This is where drinking or drug problems may develop for the tree lover of a metal woman. The female metal will usually do what is right in her view. She may take the job at the top of the corporate pyramid, ruining her own health. Governed by compassion, her tree partner will likely not be able to walk away from his partner in need. He will likely stay with her through all her injuries, and therefore her pain may become his.

Metal-woman appears more frequently in modern times
A much younger tree-man is powerless to oppose her will

If the younger tree-man is not strong enough, this may lead to drinking or drug use. He may become bitter or depressed and in the end, his liver can be overwhelmed, leading to diseases associated with injuries to the bone marrow and blood functions. Like liver cancer, these diseases take a long time to develop, so please the tree-men who are reading these pages, keep an eye on your blood pressure, which will reflect how you are coping.

As a tree, in addition to your own emotions, you are always running your partner's emotions through your bio-field, which will seem doubly strong if you receive them in connection to your metal partner who is always provocative and typically unsatisfied with the status quo. The tree lover will carry all that becomes handicapped in the relationship on his shoulders, thus constantly dealing with double or triple the amount of processing the negativity in the relationship. However, even in the clear sight of this sort of problem, the metal-woman will likely not lose her sharp edge. "You have a problem, not me," she might say. "You need to be more objective, clearly I am right in this case and in the other case, as well, and you need to face it." This is how the metal stays sharp – by always defending her actions. Just like knife against knife and sword against sword, the metal gets stronger by arguing and winning her positions.

To conclude, not all metal females are like this. We are dealing with 'tendencies' whenever we discuss the characteristics of 5-element personalities. The corporate female has just as much right to be metal as any male. Both metal archetypes have similar tendencies when it comes to relationships. Most strong metal people value the loving and compassionate traits of the tree - this is the reason they are paired up! It would be highly beneficial for the metal female to CULTIVATE WATER occasionally becoming humble, passive, and allowing tree to soften and open their heart.

Chapter Seventeen

What Turns Each Element On

Now we take another look at romantic relationships, explaining the forms of behavior most pleasant and arousing for each element engaged in a sexual partnership. We begin with the element of fire, as is done everywhere in this book.

The fire-people are often erotically turned on by anything difficult or nearly impossible to achieve. Please note the difference between the challenges a metal-lover requires to become stimulated as opposed to those of fire. For a metal, it must be challenging enough to arouse them, but also needs to be attainable, because they cannot stand defeat. However, when a fire-person engages in a sexual fantasy, it must be something really, really crazy and not necessarily completely possible, although the fire-person may end up undertaking it anyway, enjoying themselves tremendously. For instance, making love in a public space in broad daylight is not appealing to a metal lover. It is too crazy and there is really no personal victory involved. Unless perhaps the metal person's fire-lover bugs him for a while and calls him "chicken" several times, then he will go through with it. Doing it in this manner pleases the metal, because he *proves his lover wrong* while defending his reputation. Unlike the fire, who might authentically enjoy exhibitionism and does not mind being caught, the metal lover would only have public sex in such a way as to look crazy enough for his fire-girl, but in reality be completely safe and protected against everything that might go wrong. Otherwise, metal will not do it no matter how much nagging he receives from his fire-lover.

Fire-lovers love being naked and exposed so much in fact, they may find it difficult to work up a sexual appetite if the couple hides under blankets and stay in bed for most of the lovemaking. Fires prefer to have sex with lots of light and good visibility. They may wish to open the window curtains, allowing light to stream in, or choose to engage on the deck of a swimming pool or an office-desk. Just about any situation which seems taboo for other people will often be a huge turn-on for the fires.

Fires usually love unpredictable moves, twists and turns, and are internally driven to change their body postures and positions often; just as fire flames flicker and twist on a candle or in the fire-place, their bodies cannot remain still for long. Also, they are partial to changing positions swiftly, which is almost inevitably too fast or perceived as too much unnecessary movement for the other four elements. I wish to impress on the non-fire elements though that when fires remain in the same position for more than five minutes, they are bored unless they shoot straight for the orgasm (then they don't mind). However, if they are still in the process of playing and trying to build up excitement when something bores them, they may actually stop the whole thing and do it later their own way.

Fires are sometimes turned on by aggression and need to be sexually in charge at least 70-75% of the time and if they can get away with 100% of the time they couldn't be happier. Fires may enjoy doing it with impossible partners. A vast age difference, religious limitations, some disability, enormous difference in social hierarchy, all differences and distances which need to be "burned" through make the involvement of fire's love interest more likely. They want the act to be swift, bold and brilliant like the falling of a comet, although they may wish to "repeat the fireworks" over and over again - leaving them utterly exhausted.

As I mentioned earlier, fires need ample light and space in order to fully express and enjoy their sexuality. But they also need to make loud noises and be able to scream. I knew one woman whose husband always covered her mouth when she was about to scream from pleasure. That woman stopped having orgasms with her husband. Fires truly enjoy verbal communication during intimacy. They have intense urges to tell their partners what they're about to do to them and desire to hear them say something back. Fires have a pronounced need to make animal or other wild sounds as they experience the carnal pleasures, not just the screams of extreme joy as they approach orgasm. A husband, who I know as a friend, shared once that he lost sexual interest in his wife, because she could not accept his animal talk during lovemaking and for him it was not interesting to do it quietly. He confessed that only after he met another fire-lover was he truly able to understand how heavenly pleasurable love making can be. *Fires enjoy discussing what happened in the sexual act afterwards.* Usually they do so in an almost cynical fashion, meaning with lots of laughter and in an emotionally withdrawn state. The bashful water-people may cringe at this display of boastfulness and bad taste. For the fires it is almost the same as bragging about their other adventures. It puts zest in life. However, they do not enjoy after-sex cuddling when all the burning and mutual incineration is complete. There has to be freedom to jump immediately into the next endeavor, un-related to sex, such as going out to eat, sending a business email, calling a friend, going horseback riding, or just running outdoors. Just about anything is better than staying in the same room touching and cuddling for a along time after everything is finished. *Fire needs a fresh supply of wood to start burning again.*

Fire people like making loud noises during lovemaking
Trees like to cuddle afterwards, which the fires cannot stand

Let us move to those who love lingering in the afterglow of love making, touching their lover sweetly or merely watching their face transformed by love and melting on sight. Of course, they are the tree lovers. To be true, trees love sweetness, touch and all the romantic gestures of the world before, during, and after the act of intimacy. In fact, they may enjoy having lots and lots of foreplay with no action following it. Fire people may find this to be too sweet or too challenging. They may even think that the tree person who treats them like this is pretentious, insincere, or that she or he is simply teasing them for some reason. As a result, some if not all of this sweetness may not be to the fires' taste. But the tree lover wants it all! All the long hours of just holding, lying together and doing nothing but staring at each other's face provides them with a sense of safety and security, tells them they are being cherished, respected and understood, and this is essential, for the tree needs to know that they are with the right person and love can last forever.

Only if or when tree-lover is comfortably rooted in their lover's heart, will they display their mighty, quite magical, intuitive lovemaking skills. With the trees, things must evolve according to some mystical internal timing, which even trees themselves cannot understand or explain. For some unknown, totally irrational reason, one day she acts cold, saying it is too early for something serious, but then the next day, she may be standing at your door so prepared for bold leap forward in the relationship, that you her poor metal lover, remain speechless and paralyzed. Of course, she forgives you, because she loves you like an angel.

Some sexual play should never be done to the tree-lover and unfortunately these are the same acts with the potential to turn on the fire-lovers. See how confusing it all might be? You can see how helpful it is to hold knowledge of one's innate element! Things which do not turn on your

204

tree-lover but instead turn them off (even scare them) includes; grabbing them from behind as their head is in a closet, pulling their hair or arm in a forceful, but playful mood. These are absolute NO's for the trees, but definite yeses for the fires.

The tree needs a gentle, slowly growing process of foreplay. Like sensual undressing and prolonged kissing, beginning with parts of the body where they feel comfortable being kissed and gently exploring further and further. Be prepared as a lover of the tree, that moving from kissing on the lips to kissing anywhere else may take months if not years. All throughout the sexual experience there must be a secure sense of safety and trust, with both parties equally enjoying each step. The person who undertakes the difficult, yet ultimately rewarding, task of being a tree-person's physical lover must develop a certain degree of psychic ability and constantly tune into their state of sexual arousal, signs they are open for a new step, and repeatedly check in to make sure that what she/he is about to do is okay with them.

Even in the middle of the most heated sexual experience, their natural compassion, kindness and desire to sacrifice for the sake of another will dominate the tree person's sexual behavior. This is why it is such a daunting task to help them discover what and how they enjoy sex. All along, the gentle exploration must be accompanied by expressions of romantic involvement, through touching their face, holding their hand, playing with their hair or whispering sweet, soft words. As I said many times, this embrace is absolutely necessary for the trees, but can be most undesirable for the fire, who often becomes the trees' partner. Many a fire-lover prefers to shag like crazy for an hour without any sweet kisses.

The tree-persons' love making is soft, sensual, beautiful and can be prolonged. The tree person can never be truly fully satisfied, because the desire to embrace and merge into another person is so great; much like the shared root system of all the trees in a forest. For this reason, the tree person will often feel authentic sadness at the end of a beautiful love making session. And is also why it is so difficult for them to say goodbye to their lovers. Fires, who (as we now know) feel an irresistible urge to move out and away from where they had sex soon after they are finished, would do well to remember this about their tree lovers. As they trot off to their next experience, they must remember their dear tree-lover cannot swiftly change gears as they do. Even if the tree-lover agrees to go out to eat immediately after sex, it will take them a long time to transform from their spell-bound, post sexual union state. So, my dear fire friend, do not be angry at your tree-lover if they cannot place their dinner order. They are not hungry for steaks yet! Also remember that the tree-lovers are hurt worse than usual by displays of vulgar, dirty or unkind statement right after the two of you have loved each other. If you can, try to add a little bit of kissing, hand holding and looking into the tree's eyes while you prepare to move on. Fire, you will be able to forget what happened in less than half an hour, but for the trees the memory will never go away!

Unlike the trees, who often do not know how to engage sexually for their own satisfaction, because they self-sacrifice their physical and emotional needs, metal-lovers like to think they know everything they need to know about their sexual needs. For this reason, they prefer to make love according to their own set of rules. They follow "the plan" so to speak, and believe it or not, this pleases them very much, giving them a certain boost of pleasures within the sexual relationship.

For the metals, there must be something that speaks to them as a conquest, in order to overcome difficulties and reach a sort of perfection. Because of this, metal-lovers enjoy preparing for the action and if it involves good kissing, hand-holding or saying necessary words they will do it in anticipation of the next phase. When it comes to the actual sexual act, the metallic way has been modeled by Hollywood in practically all scenes involving sexual intercourse. It is here in the world of physiology completely ruled by reason, (quintessential metallic sex) we must measure our own "less glamorous" ways of being inside each other against a sex-dance performed as a professional ballet or top-notch gymnastic exercise. It may involve flawlessly shaped bodies, glistening front and back muscles reflected in a mirror and perfect breasts, legs and arms that are bent at the right angle.

For those of us who have very little metal in our biomagnetic field, this rehearsed, goal-oriented intimacy reminds us of nothing more than a good workout at the gym. Metal-lovers actually enjoy functioning like a perfect love machine. *Lots of precise, calculated movements where muscle tension is experienced and enjoyed, and tons of heavy breathing accompanied by constant self-reflection on how one's doing in the sex act.*

In truth, metals enjoy the use of mirrors for the sex action more than any other element. Metal lovers do not mind seeing the entire act in a mirror on a wall or on tape. It is the metals who drive our sexual pleasure industries that provide us with heaps of visual help and stimulation. For the metals, to see how the act is perfectly conducted is a big part of sexual satisfaction. Psychologically, this sometimes satisfies them more than the orgasm itself. It's *how* the orgasms occur that brings maximum pleasure.

Additionally – no surprises here! – the metal-people prefer everything to be perfectly timed and on schedule. So if they planned on love making to end before the 6 o'clock dinner, they make sure to quit at 5:30, thereby allowing time

*Metal lovers may get caught looking at a clock checking
to see how long they've been going or if they'll be on time*

to shower and dress, arriving to dinner on time. Metals do not actually enjoy expressing themselves through screaming or insane verbal expressions during the act of sex, like the fires. However, they do like to tell their partners what to do if it's necessary for overall improvement of the sexual experience, and they also like to boast about their sex victories afterward. Pay your attention and you might hear them saying something like, "Well honey, did you ever have six orgasms in one night before? Tell me the truth, darling, did you?" And of course, she must say, "Oh, no, darling, never! Never-never before did I have six orgasms in just one night. You and only you can make me do that..." Because if, by chance, she decides to be truthful and tell him, "When John was my lover I used to have ten," he will be less satisfied with the experience regardless of how he felt before they talked. He will start looking for a chance for revenge to hurt her feelings in return. He will accuse her of something she does not do so well and it will be true too. Her mood will be spoiled completely and she'll ask herself for the thousandth time, why they always fight right after having such a wonderful time in bed? The answer is simple. For you the sexual embrace is over for now. But metal needs a confirmation of that he was a hero, your hero, darling! So, don't be lazy or too relaxed after sex and give him his medal or decorate him some other way, because he deserves it! Also remember, if he thinks he can do better than John he will try his best to defeat John's record, and who is going to be a winner then? Think about it...Those of us who are married to the metals and think we are out of luck, we can always make them please us just the way we want if we truly understand and love the way God has created them, our metal men, our heroes. Learn how to say the right combination of words, or use the right kind of incentives and they will be so grateful to you...☺

As I said, although the metals are lacking in a capacity to be as empathic and intuitive lovers as trees easily and naturally can be, they still wish to do their best to please their lovers by doing what they think is right for them. However, our modern culture has distorted the metal archetype. Instead of showing these men as lovers who are eager to please and to do what is right for their more sensitive partners, some of the metals were transformed into a senseless love-machine. Somehow, he presses an invisible button on his pants and the hard penis comes out like a knife or a gun, ready to pierce and penetrate millions of times without tiring or stopping. This terrifying mechanical ideal of a man's sexual prowess, has unfortunately been sold to nearly everyone in this American society. It became a desirable behavior for any male while every female is expected to be happy just because she happens to have a love-making machine in her husband's body. Being able to get an erection at any time, instantly, keeping his weapon strong for as long as he chooses to, with no emotions shown and no weaknesses exposed -- these *are not* the necessary traits of a perfect lover for the millions and millions of American women. But we have to pretend they are, because this is how the macho men and the philosophy of machismo define the ideal of masculinity through rap music, movies and books. The time has come to change all this!

Let us now move to the water lover, the most mysterious of the 5 elements. By looking at these women and men you would never suspect the most amazing lover is behind that modest, humble appearance. The tell-tale for those who know will be their hair. The water types usually have long, silky, well-moisturized hair and most likely their eyes will also be telling you something of the mermaids or wizards. There will be glistening, beckoning light (but never directly) coming out of their eyes, just like the surface of water in a lake during the fairy hour, whispering of the ancient mysteries. When you encounter their gaze you feel it is true that some people's eyes are compared to dark pearls, black agate or sapphire. There is always a deeply running, hidden, suppressed or *unexpressed emotion* in the water lover's eyes that haunts us, the non-water people, forever. It is like being alongside a big lake or an ocean, wishing to know "what exactly does exist?" at the bottom, or how it would feel to be among the endless stretches of liquid power and constant shape-shifting forms that never become solid. What we are staring at is a promise of pleasures that cannot be compared to anything, except the ecstasy of deliberate drowning like in the best self-created fantasies, and of addictive, seductive, hypnotic pleasures waiting to be expressed and created.

Like other elements, waters have their own particular conditions and situations that allow them to give and receive love in the best possible way. We talked about how the tree wants to be safe and heart centered when making love, but for waters there is more. *Water lovers want to be invisible.* This means all the curtains must be drawn, all the blinds shut, all the doors closed, and crawling into the most hidden, mysterious place is complete when as much darkness as a possible hides the two lovers.

The water lovers have a special appreciation for blankets, and pulling comfortable sheets, pillows or hoodies over their bodies and heads even as they are about to get very sexual with you. These lovers may wish to cover their body completely during love making, because this is creating a sense of going more within than going out. And waters never-ever want to go out, they always want to go in deeper and deeper. This might seem an impossible thing for a fire lover to enjoy during lovemaking.

Water lovers like privacy and enjoy being under covers

Luckily, fire-lovers have the easiest time changing themselves for the sake of novelty. Since fire lovers often lead a sexually daring life, the fire may sometimes enjoy the challenge of being drawn to the bottom of the ocean. However, it is usually the water-water pairs who create the most spectacular sexual endurance, where mutual penetration can last many hours. A trained water-male can provide more than 50 full-blown orgasms for a female in a single lovemaking session. Indeed, waters are classified with the sexual organs in the Daoist belief system and they know how to govern the sexual fluids. The male water-lover can roll back the most imminent orgasm several times to allow his partner to experience her pleasures fully. This is why, once discovered, the water-person's level of physical satisfaction is nearly impossible to let go of.

The female water partner has long been considered an ultimate danger to males because she can surrender herself to him in a way no other woman can. She will surrender herself to a man to such a degree, and total dissolution of her own physicality, that he will experience what it truly means "to have her" without raping. The male's sense of self-assuredness will rise again and again with the water-female partner regardless of his outside esteem. Because the water person never demands anything for herself, the guy drowns in her selflessness wanting to find out what turns her on. But he will never discover, because water is water and being quiet is her true nature. On one hand, she allows many things and is very giving. She doesn't resist, but on the other hand, she is wiser than any man and sees him as a child, a selfish child and it's why she allows him to do these things.

The water-woman is double femininity and the mystique of the yin is truly celebrated in her. The fire woman can be pleased and will surrender in orgasm. But the water-woman *will not* be set on fire no matter what the man does and the man will seemingly never be able to satisfy her. Nor will she give her partner a visible sign like the sweet surrender of the tree-girl. Thus, in this relationship, the guy is in danger of constantly losing his heat, trying to make her sweat and scream or show other signs of being completely smashed, when she never will. This can drive metals crazy! Many Asian females are trained in the powers of the water element to passively control their husbands. No matter what the male lover does... the water female will always remain seemingly cold. This eventually cools down his Kundalini and kidney system, unless he knows a special technique of how to reignite his fire. A male lacking fire in his bio-field is classified as obedient. By letting him lose his fire through sex, a wise female weakens him and can control him in areas more important for her, such as providing financial security for her offspring. Although a male is weakened he does not go away, because he is still being ruled by the powerful fantasy of turning her on one day. At the same time, his male ego is magically put to sleep; as she lets him do it every times he wants to.

Let us now turn to our lazy, glutinous, easygoing Earth-lover. I say, "Hooray for the Earth girl! Hooray for the Earth guy!" If not for them, so many people would have a hard time getting their physiological needs satisfied. The Earth-person can have a good quality sexual relationship with any of the other four elements, fire, water, tree and metal. Besides, Earth-people truly love their physical experiences and this is what makes them such easy and available lovers; they will have sexual intercourse of just about any kind without problems. Just don't make it too extreme in one way or another.

The Earth-person approaches sex with a good dose of humor. Loving is like eating and eating is like sleeping and

214

sleeping is best when someone warm is next to you. It's cozy, it's comfy, it can be lazy and it's good. The true Earth-type does not have specific conditions for lovemaking. As long as extremes are avoided the Earth-person is happy with just about anything. The only thing that may seem like a condition or even a requirement, which must be fulfilled in order for the Earth-people to fully engage in sexual behavior, is convenience. Meaning, if a partner is a three hour drive away, the Earth-lover most likely will find someone closer in the same neighborhood, or better yet, the same apartment complex or university campus. Fire-people love challenges, Tree-people must have emotional throbbing in the heart before anything happens, but the Earth-people can make love just because it feels good and because they do not expect more than reasonable contentment from human intimacy. It is something to do, is generally good, so, why not do it?

The Earth-lovers are usually very welcoming of many different types of personalities and easily embrace all other elements through their sex. For this we must be very thankful, for if not for the Earth-lover, all of us other elements may go forever without partners. We can if we wish, make our Earth-sisters and brothers happier through our intimate relationships if we know what makes them tick. And this is what this chapter is all about - to tell you what a particular element likes most in their intimate relationships.

Do not make your Earth-lover travel too far in order to give you physical satisfaction. If the two of you do live far apart, find a way to arrive at her or his place when you need them, and don't be very fussy about the cleanliness. Otherwise, next time they may not extend their leisurely invitation to "watch a movie" because they will feel ashamed of their dirty house, yet probably not inspired enough to clean for the sake of a partner's arrival. Funny! But true...

Earth-lovers may crack a joke or be extremely laid back

Always include food with the sex ticket when your lover is of the Earth element. Earth-partners are often gluttonous, and this applies to both genders. Regardless of whether this particular Earth-person is overweight or not, find a way to incorporate eating before or after the intimacy. Do be aware Earth-people are actually very popular as intimate partners among their friends. They may not look like it, because they rarely have spectacular appearances, yet they have more regular and satisfying sexual relationships than other elements do, including the fires and metals. This is due exclusively to their very easy going character; they do not demand anything beyond what is absolutely normal or reasonable under any given circumstance, and are willing to try lots of our "tricks" and "things." They enjoy them too, provided they aren't too spooky or "coo-coo."

The Earth-lovers have a fondness – no surprise here – for a certain amount of dirt, literally and symbolically speaking. It may sound strange or may even be a turn-off for some types, but the Earths love the smell of sweat. At the very least, they act fine with it and find it to be normal, nothing to fret about, truly. They like to wear clothes until they begin to smell a little, in some cases a lot, but dislike when people tell them about their body odor, especially if they force them to change. They simply love the Earth, and I dare to insist they need that familiar, slightly Earthy, smell on their bodies just to feel balanced. They are then embraced and accepted by their own element, so to speak.

Following up on clothing, Earths do not enjoy dressing up. They practically never enjoy dressing up for sex. If this is important to you as Earth's lover, you may dress up anyway you want. Be prepared for the Earth-partner to crack a joke about the way you look, nonetheless she or he will willingly play along with your agenda, provided nothing out of ordinary is required of them in connection to this new costume or that the costume itself causes no physical harm to you or them.

Jokes may be fun for Earths as they engage someone sexually, but metals will hate this. Depending on the intensity of this humor and degree of personal sophistication in the Earth's partner, this may become an issue or not. Earths love gentle, smooth touches. They have very sensitive bellies and underarms as well as chest and throat areas. Rubbing them almost as if you are about to sculpt them gently into something pretty is usually a perfect start-up for a nice hour of lovemaking.

Because all Earths are drawn to the Earth as their own element, they may enjoy making love outside of big cities if it does not require any terribly big effort to get there. Renting a hut on a lake, in the woods or the mountains and spending time there with the Earth-person is guaranteed to enhance the overall quality of the intimate relationship. Earths love to roll in the mud, if there are ways to engage in mud-fights or mud-baths with the Earth-lover - the pleasures of mutual love will increase.

Closing Thoughts

Society's Balance of the 5-Elements

If you have read through our book this far, you will have no difficulty answering this question; which elements do you think dominate our society? Yes, it is fire and metal. This is not to say many of us do not wish for the tree, water and Earth elements to become as valued and prevalent in our social relationships as fire and metal are. This is just to share my observations with you.

I hope you have seen the movie, *The Last Airbender*, and possibly the whole set of animated episodes that proceeded it, which tell the story of how the fire-nation went on conquering all other nations, such as water-nation, Earth-nation, and so on. As I watched these episodes and the movie, I just so wished I could make one public commentary, explaining the fire-nation could draw its energy not only from fire alone, but also from metal. When you watched the movie, did you not notice it was the machines that made the fires' imperial conquests possible? All the machines and especially the big ship they use for travelling around the world are made out of metal. This makes them a Fire-Metal nation, just like us.

In the late seventies my Daoist teacher made a prediction: *"Humans are too much in love with fire and metal. They are over-structuring and over-heating themselves and this planet will have to do something just to restore the balance. All of us need to learn how to calm and cool down in all our activities, or the disaster will come, as it already happened many times in Chinese history, when the energy of metal and fire went too far out of balance."*

Industrial military complex is the firepower enforcing laws
Lawmakers and executives are the metal structure behind it

Of course, we must admit that now not only do the Western countries, but Asian ones as well, contribute to the over-use of the fire-metal archetype with social and economic development, thus raising the world-pace of over-structuring and over-heating to much higher levels.

But let us reflect, in a more specific way, on how we engage the element of fire in our social lives. First of all, let us think about what kind of people we prefer to select as our political leaders. We probably don't have to think too hard to realize we don't normally select quiet, silent people as our political representatives, because we want them to actively speak out and fight on our behalf. For this reason, just about any great politician in America is the embodiment of the fire energy. Yes, we *love* our politicians when their flames burn brightly with their fighting spirit plentifully exhibited in their speeches and character. We enjoy, and practically demand they give their audiences loud, inspirational speeches, especially during election campaigns or when things are getting tough.

There are many other ways we worship the fire element in our society. Sports, entertainment and the celebrity cult are just a few of them. When we watch sports or entertainment programs we do not expect them to be quiet and peaceful. We expect – and we are rarely disappointed -- the fire-archetype to burn most brightly and most capriciously throughout the football game or actresses' life, otherwise we are bored and do not enjoy them. We want our celebrities to burn their lives in front of us, because most of us believe we cannot live like that ourselves. So, we select and cultivate people who will do the adventurous, unpredictable, even dangerous things for us and we will watch them on the screen of our computer or TV sets. We become their fans and bask in their glory. It's like sitting by a bonfire on a cold night, except real people must ruin their lives and their health so we can watch and admire, scold and gossip about their successes and failures. Somehow, this makes us feel good inside. It makes us feel that we too are young and crazy forever.

All our teachers, speakers and performers that have a significant impact on our society and culture are strongly endowed with the element of fire. *Yet, as we collectively admire the fires that succeeded in rising to their fame, the ones who have not reached celebrity status are often subjected to punitive disciplining. Children with too much fire face strong resentment from adults, their fiery ways suppressed through medications, scolding, and punishments.* Those with too much fire in the work environment constantly get into trouble with their superiors for being outspoken and disobedient. Women with strong fire are punished by their husbands and families for being disrespectful toward men.

Please reflect on the fact that most of our society's service and market functions have been created in such a way to either cater to the fire-people's desires or provoke others into believing they too have such desires. For instance, we all burn too much light through the night, because the fire element in us loves bright lights. The fire in us also likes all that runs against natural rhythms and is difficult to accomplish. Think about it. Less than a century ago, maintaining an entire city in light during the dark hours would have been considered a miracle, but today this miracle is expected in every city we live in.

The more artificial light displayed in the darkness, the more fascinated we become and follow the rise of the fire element in us. Every visitor to Las Vegas knows this. When the nightly displays of huge commercial logos shimmer in multiple electric and laser designs along The Strip, we feel excited, and we forget to ask ourselves, "How much does this night life cost our society? What does such an intense

222

use of electricity do to our national politics? And what does it do to the animals and natural world around the city?"

Another typical fire behavior instilled in all of us regardless of our native element, is the desire for instant gratification. As you already know, fires by nature are very impatient people. Waiting kills their element and they do everything possible (even impossible) to avoid it. This form of behavior has become the norm and is highly rewarded, while people who are good at waiting (waters, trees and Earths) rarely benefit from this innate, psychological gift.

I don't have to say much to convince you that practically all our service and market industries are designed to constantly appease the impatient desires of the fire archetype. Food must be prepared really fast and served really fast too or people become angry. Learning a foreign language or how to play piano must be taught in one month or two, or people won't bother. Fires buy on impulse and strong desire, without much thought. Our store displays as well as TV and Internet commercials are designed to provoke and sustain our strong desires while dampening our thoughts about the real consequences when we buy.

Instant gratification and living as though there are no limits to our desires, characterize our society as a whole, and this as we already know, is one of the fundamental features of the fire archetype, which will burn the entire reserve of logs in one evening if not governed accordingly.

Another element we worship in our society is metal. We are not as in love with it emotionally as we are with the fire, but we support it rationally. We admire the metal's efficiency, ability to be emotionless, and its ability to concentrate on one goal regardless of internal and external circumstances. In other words, our second fascination is with machine-like functioning, which as we know, most people with the strong element of metal naturally exemplify.

Our admiration for the metallic ways can be easily illustrated through the widespread appreciation of people who are always found sitting in their offices. Regardless of how effective these people really are, we hold a belief that if people show up for work on time and are found in their respective cubicles during work hours, they are good workers. These people often get promotions and money awards for mechanically following the necessary procedures. As we increasingly develop more procedures, or as the proliferation of administration becomes our common disease, the value of mechanic, metal workers continuously picks up.

The widespread belief is we simply need more reliable, good metallic people working inside many more metallic cubicles; then everything will be done properly. But have you noticed like I did by looking at the situation at my own university, that the more a metal-element administration is brought into an institution, the more of it is still needed? It's as if the metal energy attracts itself to itself, like pieces of magnet...

Another significant way our metal fascination shows up in rules of our society is the importance of money. Money is so important to us, we believe it is able to provide the solution for every problem we have. We often think, "If only we had more money, this and this would be resolved." Don't we? When we talk about poverty we feel we need more money for the poor. When we have a national health crisis we feel we need more money for medical treatments. When we have problems with children we feel we need more money to pay for special education. And so forth.

Those with strong metal Qi are rewarded the most
Corporations want metallic workers to obtain more metal
We believe we can prosper endlessly if we have more metal

Our country's wellbeing depends on the amount of gold reserve and how much MORE GOLD we can buy with our currency. Doesn't this seem like an absurd idea – to measure people's wellbeing by the amount of yellow metal, which we cannot eat or use for protection against bad weather? Yet, this is how it is and continues to be, at least for a while.

In addition to gold, we have fondness for other types of metal and we continue using more and more of them, as our civilization continues to grow. Some experts say we have dug nearly 30% of known iron and 50% of copper reserves out of the ground and placed them on the surface of the Earth. No wonder people steal electric wires and boil them in chemical soup so they can sell copper for (apparently) good money. My teacher had predicted that eventually all known metals will significantly grow in value unless we change and place less value on them.

Our appreciation of the metal's energy is also expressed in how we generally disregard human emotions. Especially in our work environment, we train ourselves to act like little machines or robots. We try to return all our emails and calls within the shortest amount of time possible (at least we try to act like it) without giving ourselves time to think about how our returned messages affect people's lives, or our own lives for that matter. If we are professionals, we schedule ourselves all the time, giving no chance to stop to think about the meaning of it all. And we expect other people to behave this way too. Being rational, not emotional is highly valued in our work and civil environment. We expect, even demand this from everyone regardless of how challenging or painful their life or work might be. Think about it; no negative consequences result from someone being overly rational, but if someone is overly emotional, especially if the emotional behavior is recurrent, the consequences are significant. People who have a hard time controlling emotions usually lose their jobs. People who have a hard time controlling their rational behavior don't.

It is obvious we are primarily a metal-element driven society by simply looking at our strong favor of straight lines over curved ones and rectangular shapes over all other shapes in everything we build and construct. As I sit, looking around the big student center on our campus, every piece of architecture and furniture in this gigantic hall is either a square or rectangle. I don't see a single curving line in this whole structure designed for the students' fun and leisure activities.

It would not be a stretch to assume probably more than 90% of all buildings in our society are rectangular, which is as we know one of metal's favorite shapes. Our rooms and windows are rectangular for the most part. So are our doors, beds, book-shelves, and so on. One must remember, metal element favors the rectangular shape, because it makes it easier to control life locked within a rectangular shape.

Preference for straight lines comes from the same desire to control situations that demand higher speed. Moving in straight lines seems to make things work faster and therefore be easier for us. If we look at our freeways and city streets, they are primarily drawn in straight lines despite that no one finds straight lines in nature. One last note on the rising power of metal element in our culture -- Because under the patriarchal society, males were trained to have more metal energy in their character than women, this "male metallic" behavior has become the ideal for everyone who wishes to develop a strong human character. I believe we as an entire human race, are now engaging in the "male metallic" behavior by turning into a completely rational, emotionless race of conquerors and managers.

Now it is time to look at tree and water elements. It seems to me that as a society, we do not place enough value on the tree energy. Every time I walk around my neighborhood I see the disappearance of trees. Despite our knowledge that trees provide shade and oxygen, people just cut too many of them. When I ask my neighbors why they cut their trees, they say they were taking up space they needed for construction. One person told me trees can destroy property by falling on the roofs of houses or power lines. Someone admitted trees create too much dirt and create too much work from all the leaves they drop every season. "Because of them," one person said, "streets and front yards do not look as clean as we want them to be."

The element of tree is fast being destroyed on our planet, especially in our own country. It is probably being destroyed faster than the element of water, which the element of tree is dependent on. It takes hundreds of years for trees to grow, but seconds to take them down with the new power of our new metallic tools. It is funny how we have made such remarkable progress in our ways of strengthening the functions of the metal, and yet regressed in our skills to protect the tree and forest energy.

Without sounding overly negative, I wish to point out that while new buildings, filled with concrete and metal wires, appear every day around our cities, our parks are closing and spaces for growing trees and bushes around our houses are shrinking. Every day more and more of wild nature is opened for development, because when left to itself nature does not produce much metal energy. Wild nature would just sit there, quietly creating more tree energy, but who wants that, right? In our society, we know one does not become rich by looking at trees. One becomes rich by developing land and watching the amount of gold growing in

228

We cut down trees to obtain more gold
Our metallic economy has made us sacrifice crucial elements

a bank account. For as long as we remain more in love with the metal than we are with the tree, we are going to continue destroying our natural resources and the beauty of our planet. However, the ultimate balance between all the elements, for which everything and everyone strives, always prevails in the end. Remember that not a single element can rule indefinitely. When metal comes into full swing and become a complete burden to this planet, it will be replaced and completely rusted by the water. For such is the principle of the 5-elements; nothing remains the same and not a single element can indefinitely increase its power without being replaced by the next element. Since in the cycle of mutual production metal gives rise to water, water will become the next dominant energy on this planet. We can actually observe the beginning of the water element's rising and partial restoration of balance by looking at what is occurring around the globe. *Just two weeks ago huge waves demolished metal buildings along the coast of Japan.* Scientists are also acknowledging that ocean levels are rising and the number of flood disasters are increasing, striking many countries, such as; Bangladesh, Sri Lanka, Indonesia, Philippines, Australia, Brazil, United Kingdoms, and the United States continues to rise. Water comes from all directions, washing away human-built metallic structures. After water's cleansing job is done, the trees will return.

In the areas affected by flood disasters, the tree energy returns not only because people abandon flooded areas where nature begins its slow restoration work, but also because people in these areas (simultaneously across the globe) discover the power of love creating emotional bonds between one another in ways they never felt before the disaster when metallic civilization worked as it was supposed to. Just remember how people felt in this country

Metal cannot rule indefinitely
In five-element theory water overcomes metal
We must restore balance to the tree and water elements

after hurricane Katrina and you will understand what I am talking about. Notice how everyone is helping each other in Japan after their tsunami flood caused massive devastation. Hopefully, future disasters and suffering can be averted with our CONSCIOUS CHOICE to come back to nature and respect the water and tree elements - before it is too late.

There are other ways in which we begin to recognize and respect the power of the tree in our society. I am of course talking about the "green technology" and our lifestyles, which are changing as we become more ecologically concerned. On NPR I recently heard a program about a young bio-engineer who is committed to making car parts out of mushrooms. Can it be any cooler than that? And on public television I saw a program about yet another young engineer who is committed to completely replacing the plastic we use for wrapping with a new organic material which is entirely biodegradable. Amazing!

However, as we all turn "green," we must be especially mindful our old "metallic" habits do not interject into the new ways of doing things. Here is a question -- Do some people enter the "green economy" simply because it's just another way to generate more money? I'll leave it up to you, the reader, to answer this question.

In at least two aspects of our existence, the tree energy is appreciated to a good extent. These are the service and hospitality industries, and personal relationships. Think about it; some form of kindness, despite it appearing a bit fake and exaggerated, is expected of *all* people who greet us at hotels or restaurants. This is because if we don't feel good about a hotel or restaurant, we will not spend our money there. People who try to sell us things at department stores or telemarketers who annoy us with their calls, they all try to be as nice and sensitive as they can, given the true nature of the reasons why they bother us in the first place. Although some people find it to be annoying, I find it beautiful, because in other areas of our lives we do not receive anywhere near this amount of the tree energy vibration. I do not know about you, but I enjoy going out to eat. Somebody will serve me, somebody will cook for me, somebody will have to go out of the way to be nice to me, so I need it right now! These are my thoughts before I go out and I am always thankful to the people who serve me and my friends at restaurants. *But the same presence of the tree energy at restaurants also explains why some people feel they must be rude to their servers.* Getting mad at the server, who must remain kind and compassionate no matter what, might be a rude person's only chance to express the anger they have harbored for so long. Usually those who feel helpless and/or angry at their family or boss, give a hard time to the service professionals. Next time you are about to lash out with self-justified protests think about these words.

Kindness and compassion are also required for all our love and friendship relationships. If we do not receive love and compassion from our partners and friends, or if we do not give love and compassion back to our partners and friends, there is really no reason to continue these relationships. This is how it is, and I truly hope this is how it is going to be for a long time.

The tree energy is the energy of unconditional love. This is why Odin died on a tree. Christ died on a tree turned into a cross. God tested Eve and Adam by the fruit of a tree. Lakota people feed their blood to the Sun by dancing around a tree. Without the tree-energy, which vibrates at the level of all grass, plants, flowers, bushes and trees, we cannot sustain ourselves on this planet. So, people with all kinds of elements, let us recognize this simple fact and create more of the tree energy in each and every way possible!

The importance of the water element seems to be less recognized and revered in our society than it was in the past. *In many traditional societies, people of few words, slow in action and rich in wisdom were selected as leaders.* Even today in Asia, leaders do not usually shine like our "fiery and steely" presidents and prime ministers do. They seek no public attention or celebrity status and say no heroic words, and when they choose to call for action it is usually for the sake of preserving the balance.

In our culture however, people who know how to keep silent and be invisible to others are not recognized as polite, wise or even to be of good character. Some actually consider it to be rude not to talk to others while in the same room, although there may be little or nothing of importance to say. Being talkative has almost been equated with being polite and socially skillful. We express our lack of appreciation for water-element behavior when we do not reward peaceful, passive and non-aggressive behavior in our children and young adults. I am painfully aware of this as a university professor. Students who act like fires and metals and monopolize the professor's time and attention are usually more successful in colleges and society in general.

The modern day disregard for the sacredness of water has resulted in its misconceived view as merely a commodity. We use water every day in huge quantities, for showering, bathing, watering our lawns, washing our dishes and clothes, washing our cars, and so on. Households in Europe pay for the amount of water they consume, so they save more water, because it saves them money. In our society water is either free or costs so little that over consumption is rampant. As there are fewer leaders among us that revere water as the sacred source of all life, we continue to use and pollute it as if there is no tomorrow.

A new civilization will be born where all elements are valued
If our rebirth is a conscious choice, rather than nature
making the correction for us, we will be much happier

The omnipresent force of balance (set by the Creator) never sleeps. An over-use of the metal element calls for a rise in the water element. Water already floods our culture not only through natural causes, but through significant changes of our psyche as well. The Internet, or cyber-ocean, as I prefer to call it, is the quintessential expression of the watery nature of the human psyche. In the cyber-ocean, everyone communicates silently and if they do speak, the volume is regulated so no one can win by screaming their message louder. Nerds, as we like to call them, invented the cyber-ocean so they too could govern and control life, even though they lack the metal and fire so valued in leaders outside of cyber-space. They do in fact rule and control our lives, invisibly and quietly, through endless waves of information and disclosure, on the endless sites and blogs resembling under-water caves where metals and fires cannot reach. Even if they do, they still cannot rule and regulate these places. If you ever wondered why it is so difficult to instill regulations for Internet use, wonder no more; it is difficult because in all of its forms, the Internet is an expression of the water element and this is the element that is most difficult to control.

In the coming years our 'metal' will be tested. Will it manifest as lead or gold? Does our willpower (metal) get used only for the survival of our physical family... or will it get *alchemized* into gold, being applied towards **the cause** of improving life for every person? If mankind puts aside personal gain for obtaining more metal $ it is possible to develop unlimited clean free solar energy and desalination technology for unlimited fresh water. The *sharing* of these free resources can move us away from fighting fiery wars and into Unity consciousness. It is ultimately up to us to use the metal that we have been trained to cultivate since kindergarten - towards something higher. Let's do it together.